Face the Media

Practical books that inspire

Delivering Outstanding Customer Service
Gain and retain new customers and get ahead of the competition

You're in Charge Now
The first-time manager's survival kit

Make Your Mission Statement Work
How to identify and promote the values of your organisation

2-4-6-8 How Do You Communicate
How to make your point in just a minute

Stand and Deliver
Leave them stirred, not shaken

howtobooks

Please send for a free copy of the latest catalogue to:
How To Books
3 Newtec Place, Magdalen Road
Oxford OX4 1RE, United Kingdom
Tel: (01865) 793806   Fax: (01865) 248780
email: info@howtobooks.co.uk
http://www.howtobooks.co.uk

Face the Media

*The complete guide to getting
publicity and handling media
opportunities*

JUDITH BYRNE
2nd edition

howtobooks

Published by How To Books Ltd,
3 Newtec Place, Magdalen Road,
Oxford OX4 1RE, United Kingdom.
Tel: (01865) 793806. Fax: (01865) 248780.
email: info@howtobooks.co.uk
http://www.howtobooks.co.uk

First published 2000
Second edition 2002

British Library Cataloguing in Publication Data.
A catalogue record for this book is available from
the British Library.

Edited by Diana Brueton
Cartoons by Mike Flanagan
Cover design by Baseline Arts Ltd, Oxford

Produced for How To Books by Deer Park Productions
Typeset by Kestrel Data, Exeter
Printed and bound by Cromwell Press, Trowbridge, Wiltshire

NOTE: The material contained in this book is set out in good
faith for general guidance and no liability can be accepted
for loss or expense incurred as a result of relying in particular
circumstances on statements made in the book. The laws and
regulations are complex and liable to change, and readers should
check the current position with the relevant authorities before
making personal arrangements.

Contents

Preface

In this age of instant and global communication every organisation, sooner or later, finds itself the object of media attention or wants to get noticed via the media. More and more people find themselves required to talk to the media, using their personal skills and qualities to put over a corporate message.

Being in the 'goldfish bowl' of the media is not easy for anyone except the professionals; the communication techniques are different from those we use on a daily basis.

The book moves from getting an interview in the first place to controlling the way the interview goes and to knowing when – and when not – to accept an invitation to speak on radio and television. Along the way you put yourself in the journalists' shoes, and realise why they ask the questions they do, and learn how to prepare for different types of interview, from print to radio to television, from the hostile to the friendly, from outside broadcast or 'down the line' to in the studio. It should build your confidence and help you make the most of media opportunities.

Case studies take you through a variety of typical scenarios for the managing director of a software company, the PR manager of an NHS Trust and the branch manager of a charity for children.

Written in an easy-to-follow style, *Face the Media* offers plenty of checklists and short guides for busy senior managers. Illustrations include a partial transcript of a radio interview, press releases actually received in BBC newsrooms and ways to target programmes for coverage of your issues.

ACKNOWLEDGEMENTS

This book could not have been written without the ideas and help, always generously given, of my colleagues on the Media Minds team. I have watched them perform in studios all over the country and never fail to be impressed by their command of subjects, and their charm and courtesy.

My fellow-Directors at Media Minds, Peter O'Kill and Mary Small, were unfailing in their support for the development of Media Minds as a company. I have learned so much from their different interview techniques: Peter the persistent probing news man, and Mary the quintessential English rose, who knocks them for six, and not just with her incisive questions! Peter's overview of 'what makes news' is undoubtedly reflected in this book, and in our courses.

Sylvia Horn's help in getting us started as Oxford Media Workshop, before we transmuted into Media Minds Ltd was invaluable, and she set a framework, much of which we still follow today.

Rick Thompson and John Getgood have kindly allowed their respective checklists to be reproduced here, so that a wider audience can benefit from their succinct advice. Diana Morton has contributed enormously as an interviewer, but also by her thoughtful and patient feedback, and by bringing new BBC colleagues into the Media Minds circle.

Thanks are similarly due to Penny Comerford and David Campbell, each of whom developed one of the key exercises used in our training. Penny brings print journalism expertise to the team, while David makes sure we do not forget the valuable role that local and regional news coverage can perform for companies and organisations.

All of the team have demonstrated grace under pressure, warmth and courtesy at times when lesser beings would be tearing their hair out and, not least, intelligence and creativity in conducting interviews with a wide range of clients. To see how Media Minds continues to grow, visit our website at www.media-minds.co.uk

Judith Byrne

1

Getting an Interview

Why should anyone speak to the media at all?

If you – or your business or organisation – involves any of the following, you are quite likely to find yourselves in the media spotlight anyway:

- food
- health
- the environment
- children
- animals
- young people
- elderly people
- pornography
- pesticides
- accidents
- women or men
- employees
- noise
- litter
- meeting trading standards.

If you can identify with only one of the following statements, then you may positively *want* to speak to the media:

- Two or three minutes of positive coverage on local or national media would be good for my work/ company

- I heard my boss on the radio and felt he didn't make the most of the opportunity

- One of our competitors always seems to get good publicity

What are the necessary techniques to gain media coverage that will help you?

Radio and TV advertising are effective ways to reach large numbers of potential customers, yet to promote your product or service in this way is inevitably very expensive. If, on the other hand, you can get the media to come and take an interest in you, the exposure is similar, while the direct financial expenditure may be nil.

KNOWING WHAT THEY'RE LOOKING FOR

The range of items for which an interview is needed can be from news to in-depth documentary, from a light chat show to a short piece for a business magazine. What might an editor want from an interview with you?

A news editor needs a concise insert or quote for a news bulletin, or possibly a little more than a **soundbite**, but still a statement delivered without waffle. The maker of an in-depth documentary on a sensitive political subject may use only a few seconds of a lengthy interview with you, because it illustrates or proves a point that it has taken weeks of painstaking research to come up with. You could waste a lot of time with the producer of such a programme, especially when he's casting around in the early stages for leads and angles. If you are important enough to be interviewed, the publicity is quite likely to be double-edged. Be wary. These programme-makers always have their own agenda.

Assessing different interview types

The kind of interview will depend on the nature of the programme, and the reason for including you or your company. Do they need a female entrepreneur to illustrate a piece about women in business? Are they seeking an informed commentator on conservation issues, or a balancing piece to counter an interview that went out earlier?

The more you understand about the programme and its intended audience, the better you can wrap up the key messages you want to get over, in a form the editor and producer will welcome. A good media interview meets your needs and those of the programme-makers, resulting in a piece of television or radio which is entertaining and informative.

Who is invited to talk and why

There are over a hundred business schools in this country, yet you frequently find the same commentators invited to speak on current affairs programmes. Why do the same people get asked back again and again?

Their only secret is that they are willing and able to speak interestingly about a topic in a way that fits the programme's needs. Being available is the most important factor. If you are prepared to turn up at the studio, on time, when they need you, and frequently at short notice – provided, of course, you then perform well – you are almost bound to be asked back again. So don't play the prima donna. There are others willing to take your place, either because they enjoy the limelight, or because they or their employer see the value of having an amiable and well-informed spokesperson frequently appearing on telly.

Being flexible is important:

- Fit in with what they want, be prepared to do your interview outside in the rain if for some reason this suits.

- Take an interest in the constraints they are working under.

- If you can do it honestly, praise their professionalism and the programme.

And what do you get out of it? The assumption is that you have some key messages you want to use the media to convey. If you have found out how to be interesting, engaging and amusing, there is almost no limit to the number of times you can be asked to talk to the media. The art and the skill really lies in knowing how to forward your own strategic concerns through these opportunities.

So how do you get the media interested in you in the first place?

GETTING THE MEDIA INTERESTED IN YOU

Try to find a match between some aspect of your business and a particular programme on radio or television. Look through the *Radio Times* or other media guide. If the programmes are unknown to you, try to see at least a snatch of them, to gain some idea of the style and appeal.

Make a list of the ones that could be interested in you. Think of a story or angle they might like:

- Can you show someone using the device?

- Do you have a piece of film to illustrate it?

- Is there a human story of someone whose life has been improved as a result of doing your activity?

Does all this sound like doing the journalist's job for him or her? Well yes, but then if you can offer an entertaining couple of minutes, just at the point when the researcher or producer is casting about desperately for a filler, your needs can perfectly complement theirs!

Possible TV programmes to target for an innovative product to help people with disabilities

ITV 11.45 am
Sunday Link
Magazine about people with disabilities

BBC2 5.00 am daily
The Learning Zone
Business and Training

Channel 4 7.00 am daily
The Big Breakfast
Daily entertainment show

Channel 5 9.00 am
Espresso Daily
Consumer advice

Sky News
Rolling news programme

USING PRESS RELEASES

So you've got a good story about your company. How do you get it into the press, or onto radio or TV? If you're lucky you may have a good contact in the media, and he/she might use it. If it's world shattering the rest of the media will pick it up. Otherwise you're stuck with it appearing in just one place – which isn't what you want at all. Or you – or your press officers – can try cold-calling the news editors or specialist writers on dozens of papers, magazines, trade publications, and radio or TV stations. That can pay off, but it can also be a lot of work for nothing.

The most effective way of communicating to the media at large is via a **press release**. It goes all over the place, wherever you want. It allows you to say what you want. And it is relatively cheap.

You need to have a real story: what is known in the business as a **peg**. A peg, for a local paper, will be something of local interest: a local choir has had a television programme made about it, a local businessman has won a major national prize. For national news media it must always be immediate: the important date has to be a few days in the future. The reason for using your press release is that it says something genuinely new, interesting and significant.

Identifying the news value or peg

- The first/the biggest/the longest/the oldest.

- It's happened in this town/region (= coverage of local paper or radio).

- It's curious, revealing, funny or entertaining.

- It's significant; soon everyone will be doing it/reading it/ wearing it.

- It could have an effect on anyone's daily life.

- It adds something to an existing news story.

On the assumption that you have a satisfactory peg, you can draft a press release.

Writing a press release
All the essential information has to go into the first paragraph. Guides for writing press releases always advise you to answer these questions right away:

- What?

- Who?

- Why?

- Where?

- When?

- How?

FINDING THE HEADLINE

Headlines are usually short. This is a real-life example from a press release sent out by a firm of solicitors and received by BBC News:

Rescuer at Horse Show Receives Damages but is Left Short-Changed by Inadequate Insurance

---

It did not become a headline on the *Six O'clock News*!

If your press release is really well written, and the heading is easily turned into a headline, you can experience the satisfaction of seeing virtually all of your press release appear as a news item in the paper next day. Finding the heading which will appeal to the **reporter**, and more importantly to the **sub-editor**, is a skill that comes with practice. Remember the guidelines:

- if it is the latest/largest/newest

- if it can affect all of us in some way

- if it is happening now or recently or soon

you are well on the way to having a genuinely newsworthy headline.

Getting the right look

Don't forget to check the overall look of the press release:

- 1.5 line or double spacing.

- Single-sided A4 paper (one sheet if possible, two at most unless a lot of technical details really need to be enclosed).

- Use first class post or fax or courier to deliver.

- Make sure you put your name (or the organisation's contact person) and address, phone, fax and e-mail details – and an alternative if you might be away at all.

- Check the accuracy and spelling before you send it.

- If addressed to an individual make sure you have his/her correct name and title (nothing annoys recipients more than being wrongly addressed).

If you are holding a press conference make sure the details and location are set out clearly.

By all means follow it up by telephone – don't be aggressive, ask if they have received the release, have they any queries, can you help them at all, are they coming to the press conference? Leave a way open for you to ring back.

PUTTING OUT THE PRESS RELEASE

Journalists are under constant pressure to find genuinely new news stories to interest their readers. It's sometimes said that journalists are lazy if they more or less reproduce the press release you have sent them. Put the other way round, a good, succinct, newsy press release which meets all the criteria of journalism deserves to be reproduced more or less verbatim.

So what are the criteria?

1. Essential facts up front: who, what, where, when and why. Provide the answers to these questions and you have made a start.

2. Provide a peg or link which makes it instantly newsworthy to the paper or programme you send the news release to.

3. Offer a picture, or an element of human interest, and you increase the attractiveness of your story even further.

Extract from a press release

MERLIN
Photocall – April 4 200x
PUGWASH SAILS AGAIN

Captain Pugwash creator 72 year old John Ryan is
helping to launch the jovial pirate on a new adventure
this week . . . 50 years after the Captain's first
appearance in the *Eagle* comic.

Pugwash and the crew of the Black Pig have sailed
back onto TV screens in a successful new series of
animated adventures, and now he's even been pressed
into service with the UK network of Sea Life Centres.

Sea Life has spent £500,000 creating
Pugwash-themed treasure trails around its spectacular
marine life displays, and Mr Ryan is making a rare
personal appearance to christen the first one at the
National Sea Life Centre, Birmingham.

He will be joined by 30 schoolkids dressed as pirates
in a bid to solve a series of fishy puzzles around the
Centre to claim back the stolen booty from Pugwash's
arch-enemy Cutthroat Jake.

Mr Ryan developed a unique animation method
using 2D puppets operated by levers and strings for
Pugwash's debut in 1957 . . . and it worked so well the
series ran for two more decades.

Photocall
**Mr Ryan, the young pirates, a lifesize Pugwash
costume-character and a canal barge specially
rechristened 'The Black Pig', should provide a number
of good picture opportunities.**
Date: Friday April 4th
Time: 11 am
Venue: The National Sea Life Centre, Birmingham

*Issued by Merlin Entertainments Ltd. For more details
contact Mark Oakley 01202 666900.*

This press release gets a lot of things right:

- the headline sums the story up well
- there are lots of facts
- there are excellent picture opportunities
- the contact details are very clear.

Provide quotes and photo opportunities, otherwise they'll waste your time by asking for them probably at an inconvenient moment. It won't prevent follow-up calls, and do deal with them patiently even if they seem not to have read the release properly. Being helpful cuts down the chance of a journalist distorting a quote obtained over the phone, or even making one up on the basis of the contents of the release, or of you saying something you later regret in a hasty phone conversation.

Dealing with the first approach

Whether it is a print journal, a radio or TV programme, the reporter, producer or researcher will initially phone you to check out a particular story. This may just be a **ring-round** to find out more, or they may want to test whether you are a suitable candidate for interview. This can be an important telephone conversation. Try to give your whole mind to it. If you are in the middle of a meeting, offer to ring back – but do so within ten minutes. A producer trying to fill a gap will not wait around for you to come back to him.

- Make two or three colourful points; use vivid real-life examples, avoid professional jargon.
- Pause every now and again for input from them.
- Try to remember what questions they ask you, some will reappear as interview questions.

ASKING THE RIGHT QUESTIONS

1. The reporter, producer or researcher is likely to begin by giving you some idea of the nature of the piece. If they don't, ask:
   —what kind of item is this for?
2. Unless it is obvious, because they have reached you through your press office, ask:
   —how did you get my name/the name of this company?
   or
   —why do you want to speak to me in particular?

3. Later, when they have confirmed they want to use you – which may be in a second phone call – ask
   —what kind of programme is this?
   unless it is a mainstream broadcast that you can easily find out about. Try to get clear what sort of contribution they want from you.

4. Ask how long they have for your interview (and don't be surprised if the answer is as little as two minutes).
   —Will anyone else be taking part?
   —Will there be some film before you are interviewed?

Time is crucial to them, both the time it takes to put the programme together and the time they've allowed for your contribution.

Try timing the interviews you hear on the *Today* programme on Radio 4, or a local TV news programme to see how much (or little) can be said in one or two minutes.

Asking for a fee

You can, in certain circumstances, ask for a fee for appearing on radio or television. Most often this will be when you are invited to speak as an expert or objective commentator on some subject. Fees are not payable for a news interview, and unlikely to be so for a magazine in which you are able to mention your company or product. If you appear on a consumer programme to defend your

---

What you can reasonably expect when invited for interview

So that you can prepare properly, it is fair to ask what the general direction of the interview will be:

- Ask how long the interview will last.
- If it is pre-recorded, ask how many seconds/minutes will be used.
- If it's live, ask how much time for the whole interview.
- Ask whether others will appear and what their role will be.
- You can have a PR person present.
- You should not be recorded without your knowledge.
- You have the right to be physically comfortable.

---

company's record, then a fee would obviously not be available, as it is deemed to be in your interest to have the chance to defend your company's record.

If your house or office or other property is to be used as a backdrop or stage set for a television programme, then facility fees can certainly be asked for. You could ask a fee if you undertook to carry out some research and supply information not otherwise readily available. Appreciate that asking for a fee may prove a disincentive to your being asked again: many producers work on tight budgets.

CASE STUDIES

Introducing Carol
Carol, at 33, has just become Managing Director of Softly, Softly, a successful software company in a highly competitive market. She has virtually no experience of talking to the media and is inclined to be impatient when

her Communications Director suggests meetings to discuss possible media interviews.

However, the company is currently planning a move into the Malaysian market, and she is beginning to see the value of giving interviews to, for example BBC World Service or Sky or CBS News.

Introducing John

John is the 46-year-old PR Manager of a large NHS Trust covering two major hospitals. Until now he has handled most media contacts himself. His Trust is soon to be merged with another covering seven cottage hospitals and a variety of other medical services. John knows he will be PR Manager of the newly formed body. Soon he will need to field Board members on local radio and regional TV to explain the strategy and reassure about what appear to be local cutbacks. He is currently writing a communications plan for the new Trust, to be presented to the Board.

Introducing Lesley

Lesley is 51, and the Birmingham Branch Manager of a well known national charity for children. Her skills are mainly in fund-raising and people management. She has little experience of media interviews and is fundamentally distrustful of journalists and the press in general. But head office is keen that the new campaign is well publicised at local level, and expects her to front it.

ACTION POINTS

1. What three things can you do to make it more likely that you will be asked back again after an interview?

2. Which radio or TV programmes might be interested in your topic?

3. What are the most important questions to ask before you do an interview?

PREPARING FOR YOUR INTERVIEW – FINAL CHECKLIST

The following questions are not definitive and will not apply in all situations. However, if you have asked yourself these questions and feel confident with your answers you will be well prepared for your interview on radio or television. If the approach is from the press, most of these questions will still be relevant. But remember: don't be rushed, take your time, prepare yourself and call them back.

- Why do they want an interview?
- Why is it me?
- Who will be interviewing me?
- Which programme is it for?
- Will it be live or pre-recorded?
- When is transmission?
- What is the audience?
- When is the interview?
- Where does it take place?
- Will they provide transport?
- What do they want out of it?
- What will the questions be?
- What length of the interview will appear on air?
- Will it be just me or a debate?
- Who on my staff is briefing me?
- What do I want out of it?
- What are my key points?
- What human connections can I introduce?

- What should I wear?
- Who is coming with me?
- When will I rehearse?

John Getgood

2

Talking to Journalists

Before you talk to a journalist, it's worth considering the views you already hold about reporters and broadcasters.

- Do you see the tabloid hack differently from the broadsheet news hound; or are they part of the same profession?

- Are journalists proper professionals?

- What motivates them?

- Why do so many news stories seem, according to anecdotal accounts, to be distorted?

- Are journalists out to get a good story at any cost, and never mind the truth?

Understanding where the journalist is coming from puts you in a stronger position if you want to be sure they report your story accurately.

Of one thing you can be sure, the journalist is on the look out for news.

FINDING OUT WHAT COUNTS AS NEWS

> *News is people. It is people talking and people doing. Committees and cabinets and courts are people; so are fires, accidents and planning decisions. They are only news because they involve and affect people.*
>
> Harold Evans, when Editor of the *Sunday Times*
> Quoted in *The Practice of Journalism* (Heinemann, 1963)

There are (at least) three different ways of defining news. All rest on meanings of the word 'new':

1. News has just happened – or even better, is still happening. The event to be reported as news has to be new, that is to say, recent. If it happened three months ago, or even the day before yesterday, that's usually not good enough. If it goes on developing, with additional twists and turns, that's fine. Then journalists say 'the story has legs' it will 'run on'.

2. The second sense of news reflects the old adage that 'When a dog bites a man, that's not news, but when a man bites a dog, it may be!' This element of novelty, arguably, is what leads to some of the worst excesses of the tabloid media. First it was sex outside marriage, later it was gay sex, now, to be novel, the sex has to be almost bizarre. But new, in the sense of something we have not seen before, is an important ingredient of the news – the longest drought, the biggest hurricane, the coldest winter all play on the novelty of weather patterns.

3. Thirdly, there is a more subtle sense of new as 'significant': something that makes us look at the world, or ourselves or our lives, in a new way. Human cloning is news in this sense, or the discovery that Shakespeare was a Catholic who went into hiding or the long-term effects of greenhouse gases.

The importance of being new

Only a story with one or more of these elements of the 'new' is likely to interest a journalist. After all, having found a story, they have to go back to the editor and convince him or her it really is news. At least one daily newspaper employs more journalists than it needs, and receives two or three stories for every one they print. The pressure is to come up with something genuinely fresh.

News is 'the important bit' – for instance, when you have

attended an event, the one bit you repeat to your spouse when you come home: 'Jane Smith is leaving Fred', 'the council can't meet its budget', 'they're going to ban dogs on the village green'.

Thinking 'new'

It's worth remembering this journalistic mindset when you are going to meet a reporter: how will they turn your daily business into a 'news story'? In fact you can only begin to guess:

- A new product may be the first you can carry in your pocket, or the only one to appeal to older people, or the cheapest on the market.

- If you have an interesting story, perhaps it may be presented as the beginning of a trend: this is what people are likely to be doing in the future.

- Think of headlines like 'the end of shopping' or 'cutting out travel delays', something that would affect everyone's life.

MAKING THE NEWS

Where does the news come from? Which news is selected for publication, and why? Who decides the headline?

News =
Hatches, matches and dispatches

(*births, marriages and deaths*)

The biggest source of news are those events which are regular and predictable. Journalists use the **diary** to find sources of new happenings – which are nevertheless,

30

ompany has been proactive, and sent out a press
. National daily newspapers and radio and television
mmes receive literally hundreds of these every day.
o straight into the bin. Yours will survive:

's punchily written, with the main facts near the top
he first page

most important of all if it has a good 'peg'.

g is what makes a story newsworthy: the peg can be
If something is happening in ten days' time, for
e, a programme editor can put it in the diary and
include that item in a future programme. Or the
y be a development of a story already hot in the
f multiple births have been a news item, then a story
further twist: multiple births to a mother aged 50,
mple, would already have news value.
nterviewee brings the story alive, by saying what it
xe. This is the 'human interest' factor or the **TOTS**
oh over tragedy) story. In other cases, the point of
rviewee is to provide more information about the
Then, the value of your contribution may lie in your
ty or expertise. An independent expert can offer an
ve view. If a programme researcher wants to know
b title, it may be because the producer has told
hat a managing director can speak with more
ty than a sales director. The top person can also be
d to deal with more difficult and searching
ns than someone further down the organisation.

g it wrong

remember the times when a newspaper or
mme got it wrong. The *Sunday Times* published a
f Hitler's Diaries, and they turned out to be fake. A
ran pictures of Princess Diana, apparently with a
it was two actors who had been filmed. A
ntary programme was slated for recreating shots of
ing that may or may not have happened.

---

scheduled: elections, appointments, celebrity visits, the publication of an annual report, court hearings, council meetings, Select Committees at the House of Commons – all are well known sources of news stories.

Sourcing from the media

Other news media are very often used as a source, perhaps about a long-running issue on which a new opinion or new information has emerged. A story in the London *Evening Standard* often leads to follow-up news stories appearing in the next morning's radio or TV bulletins, for instance.

The process

Journalists and reporters write the copy, but what then happens to it may well be out of their hands, depending on how experienced they are. The **news editor** decides what stories will be covered, and may well also have decided which are to be given to which reporter, and what angle they are to look for. Below the news editor on a newspaper is the **copy taster**, who reads every story submitted and decides which to use. Finally, the sub-editor may rewrite part or all of the story, and will write the **caption** to fit the picture and also dream up the headline.

Well written headlines (and this is just as true of radio and TV) sell stories and sell papers. The purpose of a headline is to persuade the reader (or listener) to read the story underneath or to stop and listen.

UNDERSTANDING DEADLINES

Deadlines are always important to the journalist. On a daily newspaper the deadline may be any time up to 9 pm on the day before. For local radio straight news may be submitted up to an hour before the bulletin, but interviews need to go in at least three hours in advance. To reach a national evening news broadcast an item will have to be slotted in by 11.00 am the same day, unless it's a really major story. This is because a package will surround the headline, with interviews, explanations, a fuller report from the journalist on the spot, a piece of film and so forth.

The importance of timing

Timing can determine whether or not a paper has a scoop. Remember the *Times* report of an interview with Michael Portillo: that was an even bigger news story at the start of September 1999, in the run-up to the political party conferences, than it would have been if published at the time, in mid-July, when Portillo gave the interview – as editor Peter Stothard knew only too well.

Normally journalists have to get a story written up in time for the next edition of their paper or the lead-in time before their programme is broadcast. This is why it's so important to get back to them within minutes, or at least within the hour. If you don't they will have moved on to someone else.

For an in-depth feature the journalist may have a few weeks to play with. But then the slant or angle of the story may undergo a number of changes, and it is always possible that your particular contribution is dropped because it doesn't 'fit' any more. Keep in touch, be ready to offer ideas and material.

KNOWING WHY JOURNALISTS ARE SO SUSPICIOUS

Journalists are sometimes lied to, and often given a biased picture. People rarely tell them the whole truth, and are usually thinking of how to present themselves in the most positive light. This is why it is good journalistic practice to check out both sides, to make sure a story 'stands up'.

A more fundamental reason for being suspicious is the view that journalists, especially in Western countries including the UK, have of their role. Freedom of the press is seen as one of the guarantors of democracy. It is 'to be expected' that big business, politicians and senior spokespeople will be at pains to hide anything damaging or difficult from the public. It is the job of the journalist to

uncover the truth for the public go goes with the job.

Journalists are trained not to tal Good journalists are sceptical and look behind the story they are bei time, they are under constant pres are. They usually try to get at leas every story in order to present a b are better informed than the avera informed by reading, watching and media as well as their own.

Codes of practice

The ITC (Independent Television Programme Code, which has legal circumstances when hidden micro be used, and specifically mentions

> *The use of hidden microphones individuals who are unaware tha recorded is acceptable only whe material so acquired is essential credibility and authority of a sto itself is equally clearly of import*

BBC Guidelines require its jou aggressive, hectoring or rude, but sceptical, well-informed and not p emotionally attached to one side Remember that the journalist is a of the listener, viewer or reader.

BEING THE RIGHT KIND OF IN

There are several ways in which a name and decide you might be wo

It is precisely because, most of the time, the media are broadly accurate in what they are saying that these examples stand out so starkly. While details can sometimes be wrong, especially in the context of a breaking news story or a major accident, the broad outline is usually true.

As in any field, errors do occur. A sub-editor may go for a headline which misrepresents the truth. If two reports are read together, assumptions can be made which turn out to be false. The bottom line is, if the media consistently made gross errors in reporting, you would never believe what you read in the newspapers. We broadly do, though it has not always been so, and in some countries at some periods the general public is rightly sceptical.

Forming a good relationship with the journalist

You want complete accuracy in the reporting of your business. One way to increase the chances of this happening is by having a good, one-to-one relationship with the correspondent in your area or subject of expertise. This is – or can be – a mutually fulfilling relationship: you supply information, accurately noted. The journalist receives or confirms stories from an independent source.

The columnist or programme researcher who covers your area can become a regular contact, whose knowledge and understanding of your business keeps increasing. As a result you may find stories about your organisation are usually fairly accurate, and if there is something complex to explain, she or he will take the time to listen.

KEEPING IN TOUCH WITH THE LOCAL NEWS MEDIA

If you are part of a very large company you may feel that your time should only be spent on national news outlets, and the local media are not important. There are many reasons why this is not necessarily true. Wherever you are geographically an issue can blow up which is essentially local: your impact on the environment, a break-in or burglary, something that happens to an employee.

Local newspapers are a source of news stories for the bigger nationals, and local radio in particular feeds into the national scene. The head of news at Radio Thames Valley, or the editor of a Glasgow edition of a bigger newspaper chain, will be required to alert London to any story likely to grow to national size. But that head of news will also want to attract a little glory by being in first with the news item. If you have cultivated the local station, you can count on better understanding and some advance notice of the line they are going to take.

And don't forget, your employees live locally; they read and listen to the local media. They are gratified if positive stories come out about their place of work. Good news stories played locally can have an excellent impact on employee motivation and morale.

CASE STUDIES

Carol sees the media in a new light

Softly, Softly is about to launch a new piece of software which encourages users to examine and throw away old files no longer in use. The essential customer target is business-to-business: large consultancies, universities and others who want to get their employees to be more systematic about filing and data use. Polly, the Product Director, is trying to persuade Carol that the Filecost system is something that could be of general interest to the media.

Polly believes media coverage could lead to employees asking their employers for the software. Carol's mindset is still very much business-to-business sales, and she can't see why their PR agency should be paying good money to seek out broadcasting opportunities. Reluctantly she gives Polly the go-ahead.

One month later Channel 4's *Big Breakfast* daily show features a university professor who has made so many new and unnecessary files that his computer has slowed down to a snail's pace. Polly is shown taking the Filecost approach to help the professor clean up his system. As a result an article appears in the *Express*, with Softly, Softly receiving a mention. Sales for that month are tripled.

John needs to persuade his Board

John is currently writing a communications plan for the new Trust, to be presented to the Board. Board members are on the whole very suspicious of the media. He has to find some examples of friendly media coverage which could help the Trust's image locally.

He suddenly remembers Dr Judy Sweeting, a diminutive GP who took two months off work to walk around the entire coast of England to raise money for a scanner. She was followed by the regional TV station and then shown back at work. An outside shot of the surgery included the name of the Trust. John can use these cuttings to persuade the Board that positive publicity can build up community support.

Lesley racks her brains

Lesley's adviser from the press office has phoned to suggest recruiting a well-known celebrity to front local activities for the new campaign. He says that is a good way to generate media interest.

Lesley racks her brains, then suddenly remembers that very attractive actor who lives in a country mansion nearby. He has frequently contributed significant amounts of money to her charity and might just be persuaded to appear before the cameras, if she can demonstrate how much more money would be raised. And it might be quite fun to spend a morning discussing this with him . . .

ACTION POINTS

1. What is the biggest single source of news stories, and how can you make sure you are in there?

2. Why are deadlines so important, and what do *you* need to do about them?

3. Why is it always worth your while to maintain a good relationship with the local media?

3

Doing Radio

SEEING THE ADVANTAGES OF RADIO

Radio has a lot of hours to fill, and local radio especially is always hungry for news and stories. They need you! Radio is often more relaxed and friendlier than television.

On radio you have the listener's attention. Even if they're doing something else at the time – driving a car, washing the dishes, painting a wall – their brain is engaged, when a television viewer might be distracted by visual images.

You don't need to worry much about your appearance. Instead you can focus on:

- the content of your messages

- speaking clearly

- getting in that anecdote or story.

You can take in a crib sheet with your key messages written on it, but do not just read it out loud.

Noting the drawbacks

For local radio the audience is not large – but it may contain a lot of your friends and acquaintances! And the whole experience is good practice for television.

ANTICIPATING THE APPROACH

The first call is likely to be from a reporter who may or may not be the one to do the interview, or from the producer setting up the whole programme. They may talk for a while (in person or on the telephone) and ask you a few questions so they can judge whether you're a suitable candidate for interview before actually inviting you to take part.

If you get such a call you may want to gain thinking time by offering to call them back in ten minutes (but don't fail to do so, or the opportunity may be lost altogether). Say you are in the middle of a meeting, or just say you need a few minutes to gather your thoughts.

Use the time to prepare!

Even in this phone call they will be put off by long pauses, repetition, circumlocutory language, technical jargon. Regard it as a practice interview – an audition, if you like.

ASKING THE RIGHT QUESTIONS

Find out the basics:

- Who are you speaking to? Get their telephone number, you may have to call back.

- Which channel/what station is it?

- What's the name of the programme?

- What time is it broadcast?

- Ask why do you want *me*: would anyone else do as well?

- Try not to be flattered by the approach. Find out what they are expecting/hoping you will say.

- Ask what angle they are taking on the subject.

Find out the context:

- Is the interview to be taped?

- Is the interview to be done on the phone?

- Is it 'down the line' or from a radio car?

- Will you be in a studio where you'll be interviewed by the presenter face-to-face?

- Is it a one-to-one interview, or are you part of a panel?

- Roughly how long will the interview last?

Pre-recorded interviews
If the reporter comes to you to record a taped interview, make sure there's a quiet room to use.

- Remember, if you fluff you can ask them to start again.

You may be taken to an outside location for atmosphere, though this is more common on TV.

On the phone, down the line or from a radio car
With each of these options you run the risk that there will be a breakdown in communications or a technical hitch. The sound quality may be poor, in which case the producer will probably cut the interview short: not the best outcome for you.

On the phone from your office
Make sure you have time to think and prepare, that you won't be interrupted and that the room is quiet.

Down the line
Difficult because you have no eye contact with the interviewer, and you may find yourselves both speaking at the same time.

Radio car
Should have good sound quality, but there is the same feeling of remoteness from your interviewer.

If it's in the studio
Find out:

- How exactly do you get there?

- What time will you be needed?

- Can they send a car to pick you up? Unlikely. If not, and you have to drive yourself, ask for a parking place in the staff car park and arrive in plenty of time.

The head-to-head or disco
Occasionally, for a controversial issue, you may be asked to appear with another interviewee deemed to be from the 'opposition'.

Without compromising your own views or position, it can be very effective to find a point of agreement or understanding: 'I can see why Mr Jones is worried about that . . .' 'You and I, Lady Howe, have the same desire to improve things in this respect . . .'

Above all, remain pleasant and courteous. You may interrupt once, but if you butt in too often you will lose the audience's support. Many people switch off the radio if people raise their voices or seem to be arguing.

This is probably the most difficult radio context to do well, and requires plenty of experience. You can ask to see the introduction to the interview. Or if it's not yet written, ask what they have in mind. Ask what the first question will be, but not in so many words. You could say 'Have you any idea how you're going to start?'

ASSESSING WHAT THEY WANT FROM YOU

The kind of interview will depend on the nature of the programme:

> If it's a short interview for a news programme, they will want you to be concise. When it's broadcast, it will be edited; the interviewer's questions may be cut out; your replies could be reduced to just a few seconds. They are looking for 'soundbites'.
>
> For this reason say what you want to say and then *stop*!

If it's a specialist programme they will give you more time. You may be required to take part in a discussion. They will probably record the interview at some length and then select parts of it to intercut with contributions from other interviewees and the reporter's own commentary.

If the interview is on a technical subject, remember all programmes are also aimed at a mass audience, who will not be specialist, so tailor your language accordingly. Not too much techno-speak, just enough to sound like you know what you're talking about. The biggest mistake most people make when they talk to the media about their job is to use jargon.

Finding out where you fit into the programme

Ask:

- What are the subject areas to be covered?

- What is the point or purpose of the programme?

- Will you be on your own or in discussion with others?

- Who else is being interviewed on the same programme?

PREPARING FOR YOUR RADIO INTERVIEW

The stages of preparation are the same for all interviews – print, radio or TV.

- Work out what you want to say, and reduce it to three key messages.

- Distil down the three points into 'nutshells' or 'soundbites'.

- This is the most time-consuming part of preparation. Your 'nutshells' have to be colourful, short and snappy, and memorable.

- Rehearse your nutshells out loud.

- Find an anecdote, a story or a word picture (see Chapter 4) to match each of your three key messages.

- Rehearse your word pictures out loud.

- Write down your key messages and the word pictures on a single sheet of paper.

If it makes you feel better, take the sheet of paper into the radio studio and put it on the table in front of you as an *aide memoire*. Never read from it, just use the keywords to jog your memory.

Imagine beforehand the most difficult question you could possibly be asked; work out the answer and incorporate it neatly into one of your key points.

Local radio

Positive
Do not underestimate the usefulness of local radio to you and your company or your projects.

Not just your customers, but your employees may listen in. You can enhance staff morale with a good or amusing interview.

Your interview may be widely used. If it has immediate news value it will be picked up by national programmes. Within the BBC, local radio interviews may be re-broadcast several times, either networked across the country or inserted into national news items.

Negative
On the other hand, the local presenter deals with a hundred subjects daily; she or he will probably not be very well genned up on your topic. They may only know you have published a book, or won a major competition, but then expect you to supply all the detail.

Find out all you can about the presenter beforehand.

DECIDING WHETHER TO ACCEPT AN INVITATION TO DO A RADIO INTERVIEW

Pros

1. I know what my key messages are, what I want to say, and this is a chance to get them over to a large audience. Check out each of these indicators; put your key messages on a prompt card – and go for it!

2. It will take only half a morning to reach as many as 100,000.
   If this is really true, it's worth the investment of your time and energy; give the best performance you can!

3. The audience contains potential customers/people I want to influence.
   Are you sure about this? What do you know about the programme's listeners?

4. It is likely to be the first of several interviews, so if it turns out well, it will build up my confidence for a TV interview.
   Make sure to do a bit of evaluation afterwards. Listen to the tape; listen to the **questions** you were asked. Use the experience.

Cons

1. We are not quite sure yet how to describe the main points of our new product/new strategy.
   Either get this clear, cancel/refuse/try to postpone.

2. I could screw up, and if the MD is listening, or even just hears about it . . .
   If it's really important, perhaps you should go on a media training course.

3. My staff will listen in. I may make a mess of it.
   On the other hand, if you do it well you could raise morale.

45

4. It will take up half a morning.
   Weigh this against the number of people you may
   reach, and whether they include those you are targeting.

5. It's only local radio, and my key messages are aimed at
   a national audience.
   But have you got a national invitation? If not, this may
   be your only chance to interest anyone in the media. It
   could lead on to further interviews closer to the kind of
   audience you're aiming at.

6. I don't know the subject very well; I may not be the best
   person to do the interview.
   Suss this out: do you need to prepare more? Should it
   be your boss rather than you who does the interview?
   Or are you in fact 'the best person'?

KNOWING WHAT RADIO CAN OFFER

Ninety per cent of over-15s listened to radio at least once a
week in the first quarter of 2000. In the same period nine
million listened to Radio 4 and six million to Radio 5 Live.
The BBC has 51 per cent of the domestic radio audience
and a global reach with the World Service. (Source:
RAJAR/RSL)

Targeting a business audience on the radio

Programmes where a business audience would listen in:

- *Morning Reports* BBC Radio 5 Live 5.00 am daily
- *World Business Review* BBC World Service
- *News Talk* Radio 5 Live 10 pm Tuesday

To reach potential customers you might target:

- *Asiafile* Radio 4 Saturday 11 am
- *Woman's Hour* Radio 4 10.00 am every weekday
- *You and Yours* Radio 4 12 noon every weekday

An in-depth programme might approach you for an interview, for example:

- *Analysis* BBC Radio 4 Thursday 8.30 pm
- *Costing the Earth* BBC Radio 4 Thursday 9 pm

A special interest programme could also give you good coverage:

- *Money Box* Radio 4 12 noon Saturday and Monday
- *The Learning Curve* Tuesday 4.30 pm

The *Jimmy Young Show* BBC Radio 2 every weekday. Experienced interviewees always praise Jimmy Young as a thoroughly professional, well-prepared and yet penetrating interviewer. Jeremy Vine, who follows him, comes straight from TV news. Don't be put off by the light music context.

Revising the points

- Ask plenty of questions before the interview.

- Always go into an interview fully prepared with your key messages.

- Weigh up the pros and cons before turning down a radio interview.

CASE STUDIES

Carol doesn't get to wash her hair
The major software company in the States has just received a negative ruling in an unfair competition case. The issues are quite complex for the general public, but extremely familiar to Carol. The press office tells her that the local radio station wants someone to come in and front a phone-in on the issues. Carol is not sure this is a good use of her time, but the press office seems to see it as an excellent opportunity for cementing good relations with the local media.

Carol was looking forward to an evening in with her husband, they see little of each other. Because of the preparation needed there is no point in her leaving the office, she might as well go straight on to the local radio station in time for the start of the programme at 7.30 pm.

John thinks very quickly

A senior consultant in one of John's hospitals has just published a paper in *The Lancet*, on recovery rates from strokes of ex-smokers. *The Guardian*'s health correspondent is interested in doing a short interview with Dr Marek. John wonders why, and what the angle is likely to be. As he is on quite good terms with the journalist, John calls him back and says: 'I'm sure I can persuade Dr Marek to talk to you; can you give me some idea of the news value as you see it?'

It turns out the correspondent has not yet seen the article, and is rather expecting it will provide a defence for doctors who think ex-smokers do not have the same right to treatment as non-smokers. In fact, as John knows, the research points in quite the opposite direction. Ex-smokers, that is to say those who gave up smoking some time ago, have a much better recovery rate.

John thinks very quickly about how to interest the *Guardian* hack in this angle. Dr Marek is actually voluntarily running a stop smoking clinic, and apparently, far more women, and younger women, are coming along than ever before (John knows *The Guardian* targets younger women readers). Would the correspondent like a photo of Dr Marek in his clinic, as well as an interview?

The bait is successful. All that remains is for John to ensure Dr Marek will agree to the interview, and will avoid any pitfalls in answering questions.

Lesley surprises herself

Lesley has been pushing the need to talk to the media to one side. She is very nervous about making a mistake, saying the wrong thing, or annoying head office by turning down invitations at the last minute.

Tom, a young man from the press office, has come to spend a day with her, practising for a local radio interview he has fixed up. She discovers that he is very personable, appreciates the work she does in Birmingham, and agrees with her view of the main points she should get across. They practise with a tape-recorder, and she is surprised to find at the end of a morning that she has actually enjoyed the whole thing! Tom says she is 'a natural for local radio'.

ACTION POINTS

1. How can an interview on local radio benefit your company or organisation?

2. How can you best assess what a producer wants from your interview?

3. What preparation would you undertake before a panel or discussion-format programme?

4

Getting Your Messages Clear

BEING PREPARED

The most common mistake made by first-time interviewees is to estimate the importance of a media interview according to the time it takes to do. You may only be in the studio for ten minutes; what is actually broadcast may last only 45 seconds. Yet the impact can be very great, if half a million people hear it, and a thousand or so remember parts of it, or hear or see a report of what you said. Even more so if six of those people include your competitors or significant players in your business world – a senior civil servant in a government department, for instance.

This is why preparation is key. A well-prepared 45-second soundbite is more likely to be understood and remembered or even repeated. And if you have prepared it, your key message will be wrapped up in the soundbite.

But how do you prepare?

At Media Minds we once trained two individuals who turned out to be excellent spokespeople for their companies. However, at the beginning of the first day, when we asked them what sort of preparation they had undertaken, they fished out of their briefcases reams of paper covered in a long list of anticipated questions they believed interviewers might pose. A good deal of work had gone into thinking of every possible angle an interviewer might take.

'Fine,' we said, 'and what are the key messages you will be wanting to get over?' They looked a little crestfallen, for that had not been part of the preparation so far.

Instead of thinking positively about what these two bright and enthusiastic ambassadors for the company would say, all the corporate effort had gone into building defensive replies to imagined difficult and sabotaging questions from the journalist.

This has two drawbacks if it is the only form of preparation:

- it puts you on the defensive right from the start

- and it misses the opportunity to say the things you as a company want to say, right from the start of the interview.

The preparation process

Anticipating all the questions you might be asked is a very good *start* to preparation. Of course it is sensible to assume the question that will be posed is the one you would *least* like to hear and work out the answer.

There are several more stages to follow after that, however.

Having come up with all the questions you might be asked, from the simple and easy to the more difficult and challenging, you then need to work through the preferred correct answer to each: 'correct' in the sense of corporately agreed. You may be surprised to find that, even internally, there is not perfect agreement on some of the most gritty policy questions. It is vital that all your spokespeople are 'singing from the same hymn sheet', otherwise you lay yourselves open to someone spotting and exploiting key differences.

It is also useful to identify the jargon you use everyday at work, the in-house code that creeps into your speech on a daily basis. You may actually have to rethink what you mean by specific terms and try to find new, more self-explanatory words and phrases.

KNOWING YOUR STUFF

Generally speaking, you are invited for interview because you are in some sense an expert. Therefore you must know your facts. It is surprising how we all skate along, even in our professional lives, without detailed, accurate facts and figures. In your position, whatever it is, you are responsible for knowing the precise facts, and having them at your fingertips, at any rate for the duration of the interview.

And more is required: if you are in a rapidly changing situation, you must also know the latest news on your subject. (Worth asking your interviewer, as a last resort, whether anything else has happened: newsrooms are the first to know.)

The next stage of preparation is therefore to bring yourself fully up to speed on all relevant aspects of your work or topic.

Being both personal and political

In a typical corporate interview, where you are talking about your work, your company or organisation, you have to get two fundamental things right:

1. The corporate message.

2. The words you are going to use to put it over.

GETTING THE MESSAGE CLEAR

First, the corporate messages must be crystal clear, for instance:

*   Why we are launching this product now.

*   What we can say about our corporate financial performance.

*   What we want to say about our future strategy.

- How we explain any difficult or negative stories from the past.

- What our price is going to be/when we can reveal it.

- How we estimate the efforts of the competition.

- How our developments relate to recent news in the sector of the economy.

- How what we are doing relates to government policy in this industry.

And so on and so on.

This is the 'political' part, in other words it cannot be determined by the individual spokesperson, but is the outcome of corporate meetings and discussion. It must be clearly stated and rehearsed: a highly polished set of statements put over with some inherent consistency.

Speaking to the different audiences

It is unfortunately only too easy to be pulled several ways in an interview, if you let yourself think of the different audiences who may be watching you or hear about what you said. Just to name a few:

- your mother

- your immediate boss

- the leader of the trade union at work

- the workforce as a whole (especially if redundancy or closure is on the cards)

- civil servants in a relevant government department, who will receive a transcript if it is significant enough for them

- your neighbours

- your company's major competitor

- the chairman of the company

- his wife

- a local radio programme which decides to follow it up

- your boyfriend.

Some media trainers will advise you to research the programme beforehand, to see what kind of audience it has. While it is a good idea to know which groups the programme is aiming at, the producers know that on the mass media – radio and television – there is always a large casual audience made up of all sorts of groups. For instance, audience research has shown that up to a quarter of those watching daytime television actually work full time! (Some are shift workers, but others are waiting in garage showrooms, at home sick, or for one of a thousand reasons briefly watching the box.)

Honing your message
The best approach is therefore always to hone your messages so that they appeal to the most general audience possible, but contain enough new and interesting material to capture many groups. You cannot just address some of these possible audiences. What you say has to 'fit' and to make sense to all of them. And because you want to speak to each viewer as an individual, it is worth imagining here your own special listener (see Chapter 7). If you can appeal to that person, chances are you have also kept the attention of all the other viewers.

Matching the messages to your personal style
The second element is you: your language, the way you come over. It is you as a person who is putting over the message. You need to project yourself a little more than usual, as if you were on the stage or giving a speech. Display more vitality, adopt a little more authority than you would in real life. Controlled enthusiasm should be your watchword!

GETTING ACROSS YOUR KEY MESSAGES

The maximum number of key messages you can hope to
get over in any context is three. Four is too many to
remember. Think of 'Up, up and away' or 'Faith, hope and
charity, but the greatest of these is charity'. Add a fourth,
and confusion arises in the mind. Sometimes just two
messages may be quite enough, and carry greater weight
and dynamism, think of 'Jack of all trades and master of
none'; 'The quick and the dead'; 'Better late than never':
succinct messages with just two ideas.

Finding your key messages

1. The first step is to work out exactly what it is you want
   to say. That may well be largely based on the agreed
   corporate messages. Write them down as a list of
   statements. You'll find there are far more than three,
   perhaps 13 or even 23. Don't worry, just get them down
   on paper.
2. Go over them and get rid of unwanted or extraneous
   material.
3. The next step, quite simply, is to turn all these
   statements into three key messages. This is the distilling
   down stage. In order to get to a maximum of three you
   are going to have to cluster your statements under three
   headings. Do not try to rush the clustering process.
4. Each key message should be capable of being reduced
   to a headline: a new product which will clean your hair
   without you having to wet it might be advertised as a
   shampoo for people in a hurry.

BEING FLEXIBLE

A point to remember is that, as an interview takes the
form of a conversation, you can never be sure that the first
question you are asked will correspond to your first key
message. It may be more suitably answered by your third.
You cannot necessarily get your points out *in the order* in

which you first thought of them. This is why you have to be flexible, and have to stick to only three main points. Once you have got the third point over, you have only two more to deliver, and it's then a matter of fitting your points naturally into answers to further questions. Later we will see how you can try to ensure that the questions help you do that.

BEING READY FOR THE UNEXPECTED

Paxman *v* Kissinger

In June 1999 Dr Kissinger appeared on Jeremy Paxman's Radio 4 programme *Start the Week*, to promote the latest volume of his memoirs *Years of Renewal*. The interview did not go quite as Kissinger seems to have expected. Paxman began by calling Dr Kissinger the most famous diplomat of the last 30 years, but then accused him of 'rewriting history'.

Paxman noted that Dr Kissinger had won the Nobel peace prize for negotiating an Indo-Chinese Settlement in 1973, but proceeded to ask 'Was there any part of you that felt a fraud in accepting it?' and then referred to the huge loss of life after America's bombing of Cambodia. Dr Kissinger lost his cool, saying 'Come on Mr Paxman, this is 15 years or more back, and you at least have the ability to educate yourself and not lie on your own programme.' Soon after, background noise indicated Dr Kissinger was leaving the studio, and Paxman called goodbye after him.

The BBC said in a statement that the 'challenging conversation' had 'made fascinating listening'.

Based on a report in *The Independent* Tuesday 29 June 1999 p. 7

Remembering your key message

It is all too easy to talk fluently in an interview, but to forget something as simple as mentioning the name of your company. Media Minds gave a talk to a group of paperback writers, and several authors admitted they had done quite lengthy radio interviews, but forgotten to give their own name or the name of the book they were talking about!

CASE STUDIES

Carol learns to cluster

After the Board meeting Carol meets with Michael O'Kenna, the Head of Communications for Softly, Softly. The Board has approved Michael's communications strategy, and the next stage is for Michael and Carol together to focus on key messages for future media interviews.

The process takes much longer than Carol anticipated, mainly because there are so many messages she wants to get across: Softly, Softly is commited to e-commerce; it's a leader in innovative software products; the new database programme is superior to anything produced by Microsoft, according to a new objective report. Softly, Softly's unique selling point is its tutorial programmes which can be played as a video or CD, so that complete beginners new to computing can quickly get up to speed on quite complex programmes. After a whole morning of Carol saying 'but we must mention this' and 'we can't forget that', she starts to agree with Michael that a process of clustering is essential. They finally come up with three key messages, the third of which is specific to the products:

- Softly, Softly has been designing software longer than anyone else; two of their key people were involved in the original work for a well-known software giant.

57

- Softly, Softly has been first in the field with three completely new software applications, namely . . .

- The new product is special because . . .

Clustered within each of these are all the other messages Carol is keen to get over. They can be 'unpacked', as time permits, in interviews.

John defines three clear messages

John knows the Trust and its work very well, and has been through two or three management changes and alterations to the communications strategy and the 'strapline'. Due to a recent hospital scare in which a number of elderly patients died while waiting to be removed out into community hospital beds the current strapline 'Care in the right place at the right time' seems inappropriate, as it might be regarded cynically by some.

However, John is pretty clear about the three key messages everyone should be trying to get over when they have the chance. The South Tenterden NHS Trust wants to be seen as:

- Listening to the community.

- Offering care as near to home as possible.

- In the context of a modernised health service.

The next step is to think up some nice soundbites to encapsulate these messages.

Lesley discovers why her charity is unique

Lesley has just undertaken an analysis of the competition. There are so many other children's charities, it is really important to be able to pick out what Children and Parents stands for uniquely.

Lesley particularly likes Children Nationwide, which describes itself as the only charity which funds research into diseases affecting children. She thinks perhaps her charity is special and unique because it is the only one that cares for the needs of the parent as well as the child after family disasters. This will be one of her key messages.

ACTION POINTS

1. Knowing what you want to say entails getting your messages clear.

2. There are two parts to clarity: the agreed corporate messages, and the way you put them over in your personal language style.

3. Cluster all the things you want to say into just three clear messages.

5

Turning Messages into Soundbites

From the point of view of a programme producer, the ideal interviewee is someone who can communicate novel and interesting ideas in a few succinct phrases: someone, in other words, who can come up with a soundbite. Politicians do it daily, and some presenters seem to do it naturally, almost without thinking.

How do you turn your message into a soundbite? One way is to think of it as creating a picture with words, so that the picture pops into the mind of the listener or viewer you are talking to.

CREATING A WORD PICTURE

She was born in a cave amongst rocks in the mountains. Her body was as thin as a stalk of straw, but her head was as large as a thimble. The witch took seven years to grow up; during that time a cat told her stories which were full of evil and hatred, and so malice grew in her heart.

As you read that paragraph, does your imagination build a picture in your mind? The essence of a word picture is that the listener's imagination gets to work so they are *engaged* in what you are saying.

Word pictures are an essential aid to being understood by your listener. Painting a picture in words is vital on radio, but it can also help on television. A vivid word picture can help to convey a complex message. Here is a

partial transcript of an interview which took place on the
BBC's Radio 4 *Today* programme.

CREATING WORD PICTURES WITH JOHN HUMPHRYS

The whole interview takes only three minutes. The
interviewee, Ian Redmond, with a little help from John
Humphrys, manages to explain, or perhaps more
accurately remind listeners of, the Darwinian principle of
survival of the fittest. Redmond wants to describe what is
happening to elephants in Africa and Asia, and to promote
his organisation, the Convention on International Trade
and Endangered Species. (This title is quite a mouthful, as
you can see, yet Redmond does successfully manage to
work it into one of his answers.)

Redmond also uses vivid word pictures, and when he
uses statistics he explains them and puts them in context.
He describes **trends**; he uses **analogies** – three in all. He
tells a **story**. He keeps his language **simple**.

John Humphrys works with Redmond to produce an
entertaining and informative interview. It is very much a
joint effort. Starting the interview off, Humphrys gives the
headline:

'*Elephants are fighting back against all the poachers
who're killing them for their ivory tusks. **They are stopping
growing tusks**.*' (This is the **headline**.)

Redmond then uses **statistics** effectively. He says:

'*instead of one per cent tuskless . . . now as high as 30 per
cent in some herds.*'

Note that little phrase *as high as* so the listener knows
how to estimate the importance of the figures being
quoted. Redmond says:

'*It's evolution in action . . .*'

Humphrys immediately jumps in to help develop the
notion of evolution. Taking the role of the intelligent
listener, he protests:

'*But I thought evolutionary changes took hundreds if not
thousands perhaps even millions of years . . . ?*'

Redmond sees the point and immediately joins in:
'*Do you not remember from your school biology . . .*'
'*Not a lot,*' says Humphrys, cheerfully.

This is a good **joint interview effort**: they are both
'teaching' about evolution.

Building on that base, Redmond starts again. He
mentions '. . . *the* **story** *of the peppered moth.*' It is always a
good tactic to promise to tell a story. Your listener, driving
a car or sitting in a railway carriage, is happy to be
entertained. The listener likes a story: his or her ears prick
up, and just for a moment you have a captive audience.

Redmond then speedily explains that the dark form of
the peppered moth became more common in the 19th
century, because the dark moth was better able to hide on
all the sooty tree trunks produced by the industrial
revolution, and in fact this happened in only one
generation.

Just the phrase 'the sooty tree trunks' is a word picture,
that is, it conjures up an image in the mind's eye.
Humphrys promptly brings in another evolutionary idea:
'*Ah. Camouflage,*' he says.

The story of the peppered moth is an **analogy**, what
Redmond calls '*An exact parallel.*' He instantly goes on to
find another:
'*If you want to compare it to someone breeding rabbits,
say 200 rabbits, 198 of which are black and two of which
are white, and you breed the white ones and kill all the black
ones, obviously you'll have a white population . . .*'

Redmond then brings it back quite smoothly and
naturally to the main subject of the interview, elephants:
'*What the poachers have been doing is eliminating the
elephants with the biggest tusks.*'

John Humphrys helps again, '*Ah . . . I see!*'

And Redmond continues, with a third **analogy**:
'*In an elephant society, if you're a male you beat off the
other males and get the girls and if you're a female, you're
more successful at protecting your young . . .*' Note there
are two **word pictures** here.

'*Tusks are not just ornaments for elephants.*'

Note the **simple language** Redmond tries to use.

'If the advantages of having a tusk are outweighed by the disadvantages of being shot by poachers, then the tuskless ones'll suddenly have an advantage.'

Humphrys comes in: *'So is it possible we might end up with elephants without any tusks at all?'* As interviewer he is helping to explain, or re-explain, to ensure the listener 'gets it'. You will often hear interviewers working quite hard to clarify a point made, perhaps rather fuzzily, by the interviewee.

In fact, if you're frequently interviewed, you can sometimes find that your interviewer has, on the spur of the moment, come up with an excellent word picture you can then use yourself in later interviews! Most journalists, after all, are wordsmiths, and very good at encapsulating and re-presenting others' ideas.

At the very end Redmond manages to mention, again quite naturally, an **acronym** (which he immediately explains): CITES: the Convention on International Trade and Endangered Species. He demonstrates by an example what CITES is for: *'(The) ivory ban in 1989 meant there was a drop in poaching in Africa and Asia, but now there's an increase in the price of illegal ivory, and so poachers are setting to work again.'*

So in summary, in the space of a three-minute interview Ian Redmond, with some assistance from Humphrys, has:

- explained a complex natural phenomenon in the context of principles of biological science

- mentioned the name of his organisation

- and shown what worthwhile things it does.

KEEPING THE LANGUAGE SIMPLE

Why *not* be simple? All our trainees worry at some time about reactions back at the ranch if they simplify too much. What will their colleagues think if their complex work is presented in a dumbed-down version? In fact, if you succeed in painting a picture of what you all do, within the constraints of a media interview, they are more likely to admire you, and be glad they have so effective a messenger. And if you manage to:

- attract attention by using the word 'you'

- keep interest by using vivid visual examples

- leave a lasting image

then no-one will complain you have oversimplified.

If you are an IT specialist talking to the editor of a specialist new technology journal, you may well feel you don't need to simplify things, because he understands the subject as well as you do. *This can be a mistake.* By easing into your familiar professional jargon, you are employing a sort of shorthand, and effectively leaving it to the journalist to decide how to present your story to the public.

Even with such a sympathetic and knowledgeable interviewer, there is a danger that what will be highlighted is what interests the journal, and the message *you* wanted to get over never comes through.

If you have worked out beforehand what your simple messages are, you can state and reinforce them, using that language and the attractive and memorable examples you have come up with. This actually helps the editors do their job, for they have to come up with the eye-catching questions and stories which will take their readers further.

Can you be simple?

Some subjects seen so complex, even to those working on them – innovative technologies, complicated scientific advances, medical techniques – that distilling them down into soundbites seems well nigh impossible.

A quick rule of thumb: if you had to explain your work down the pub, or at a dinner party, how would you put it? You would probably pick out the most newsworthy element: what changes in everyday life it could lead to, the fact you're ahead of the Americans on this, the benefits for a particular group of people. That's probably the best angle to start with, even if you have to qualify it a little.

'In five years' time it could mean . . .'

'The Americans are also working on this, and it's a matter of who gets there first.'

'The benefits for newborn babies could be tremendous, though of course not for some time . . .' and so on.

TELLING A STORY

It is possible to turn even the most ordinary set of events into something resembling a story. The techniques are as follows.

Describing the 'before' and 'after'

The 'before' contains a problem or something undesirable. The 'after' resolves the problem or comes up with some change or resolution somehow satisfying to the listener.

Product launches fit well into this scheme. For instance, BT painted a picture of evening time conflict in households where teenagers wanted to be surfing the internet while at the same time parents made family or social calls on the telephone. With only one telephone line, there was frustration and disagreement. BT's new Home Highway solved the problem by using one line to do both.

Using human interest

Your managing director may be a headline-maker in herself: 'The first woman to . . .' or your team may work particularly well together because they have dispensed with formal workwear. Recently a high tech company got a large spread about themselves, chiefly because they had a stunning photograph of people working in an office where the floor was completely covered in artificial grass.

A team pulling through difficulties with a charismatic leader, or alternatively working well as equals, can form a storyline with plenty of human interest. Or a tiny British company beating off competition from a much larger rival can be a modern-day version of David and Goliath.

USING STATISTICS EFFECTIVELY

Just think how many headlines depend on a dramatic statistic:

— Half of all women think having a baby jeopardises their career prospects
— One in three children have been bullied at school.

Knowing your stuff means being able to come up with a couple of very telling statistics, sharply focused, so that the viewer will retain them after you have finished speaking. Not only do you need to keep the figures simple, you should also indicate what you mean in words and tone. *'Nearly twice as many people in Britain are now officially obese as ten years ago: that's a huge increase'* leaves no uncertainty as to the meaning of this statistic.

Even on radio, where you have the listener's ear and brain, statistics should not be more complex than the average listener's ability to do mental arithmetic. It's usually best to offer an explanation in words as well as figures. And always round the figure up or down to the nearest whole number.

KEEPING IT SHORT

A working rule to keep in mind for broadcasting is three words to the second. In two minutes, you might be able to speak as many as 360 words. Keep your answers fairly short: 30 to 45 seconds is long enough. That will give the interview pace, allow for more questions.

Remember, media interviews do not give you enough time to explain. It can sometimes be better to start with your conclusion and only then bring forward the evidence to prove your point.

AVOIDING JARGON

Every workplace has its jargon. Medics and horticulturalists use long words. Scientists and technicians use words nobody else understands. Bankers and economists think of money very differently from the man or woman in the street. These are the more obvious jargons. Any kind of shorthand used by people in the same line of work tends to be opaque to the rest of the world. As a group, you may not even be aware how much special language peppers your talk. Try out your interview on an outsider, or maybe even a young relative.

- Go through your planned messages systematically, weeding out any jargon.

- Then re-find the simple everyday style anyone can understand.

If you have used an acronym, always explain it. Very few are known by everyone – worldwide, perhaps only 'BBC'. If part of the point of doing the interview is to get your company name known, you may feel the acronym for it has to be used – but don't say 'M & S' when the household phrase is Marks & Spencer. Always explain initials when you use them. If you can avoid them, then do.

PREPARING THE SOUNDBITE AND THE NUTSHELL

'In a nutshell Miss Smith, can you tell us your organisation's position on . . . ?'

A nutshell, in this sense, is a very succinct, but also colourful and memorable, phrase or sentence summing up one key message.

The penultimate stage of preparation is working out a spellbinding, never-to-be-forgotten way of encapsulating each of your key messages. Only you can do this, because it should be words that naturally come out of your own vocabulary and way of talking. If a word picture is built in,

all the better. Again, don't skimp this stage; a good
nutshell can become a good soundbite or a good headline,
to use again and again. It can stand you in good stead
through a series of interviews.

Rehearsing your nutshells
The final stage, of course, is rehearsing your nutshells out
loud. Make sure you can say them without stumbling over
your words. Practise them in the shower. Become so
familiar with them before the interview that just one key
word will be enough to evoke the whole phrase. That way,
you will have no need of a crib sheet. Three words are all
that's necessary, scribbled on a card if you must and in case
you panic or totally forget everything in the heat of the
moment.

Being enthusiastic
Let the excitement of what you do come into your voice,
your expression, your body language. That way, even if the
odd word or phrase is missed, the overall impression is
created of a positive person doing something worthwhile
and life-enhancing. (If you're not enthusiastic about your
work, and can't even pretend to be, question whether you
should be giving a media interview at all.)

CASE STUDIES

Carol's little purse
Carol's company Softly, Softly is about to launch a new
product which does not yet have a brand name. It is a piece
of software for paying costs of downloading items of
software products from the Softly, Softly website, in a way
that is guaranteed secure. It is distinct from a number of
other products also in development, and she mustn't say
anything which could either contravene trade descriptions,
or give away too much to her rivals about Softly, Softly's
product strategy.

  She needs to find a way to describe the product which

makes its function clear, without offering too many hostages to fortune in the future. It also has to work in the far eastern market targeted by Softly, Softly.

Making use of a few good ideas from the PR company, Carol comes up with an analogy. As a prop she brings into the TV studio her own little handbag purse made of eelskin, 'my favourite object', she says. The new product will also be an 'e-purse' or an 'e-clip purse'. Using this word picture, she can also conjure up images of the kind of new shopper who will be using it.

John picks out the exciting bits

John has persuaded the local news channel that some research on bedsores could actually be of interest to a wider audience. There is the chance to field one of his Medical Directors on an early evening news programme, but with only two minutes of airtime. The Medical Director would much prefer to talk about some more complex research on human tissue, whose results are dependent upon two or three years' further study on the human genome. Either story could put St Erwin's Hospital in a good light, but the one about bedsores is more colourful, as it involves a rivetting description of how motorcycle outriders from a base in Wales can ferry a vacuum flask of gel containing maggots to any hospital in the country. Fastened onto decaying flesh the maggots can bring relief to patients who may have suffered for weeks, in as little as 24 hours.

All that remains is to coach the MD in the bedsores story, in which St Erwin's can rightly claim to lead the whole country.

Reluctantly (because he is much more excited by the human genome project), Dr Carter agrees to do the maggots story this time, provided John promises to find him a slot on a late-night Radio 4 programme to talk about what really interests him!

Lesley brings in human interest

Lesley's charity is starting to fund-raise for travel grants
for parents in poverty because of family disasters.
Payments for car hire or taxi fares seem difficult to make
sound worthwhile, until Lesley hits on the idea of showing
the difference it can make to one family.

Mrs Smith is living in temporary accomodation, after a
fire started by her husband burned their house down. She
has managed to hold on to her job in a small town ten
miles away, but after the fire the journey to work by public
transport and a half-mile walk takes one-and-a-half hours
each way. Thanks to Children and Parents, Mrs Smith's
journey times are now reduced to 25 minutes each way by
use of a hire car, and she is able to spend more precious
time with her three children, one of whom was badly
burned in the fire.

Photographs and a video clip of the Smiths at home, and
Mrs Smith being collected by the car, are turned into an
attractive package for a regional magazine programme.
Even without the visual aids, a word picture can be painted.

ACTION POINTS

1. Keep the language simple.

2. Try to tell a story.

3. Create some word pictures.

4. If you use statistics, put them in context.

5. Use analogies, especially if you have something quite
   complex to explain.

6. Always explain any acronym immediately you use it.

6

Feeling Confident

BEING PREPARED PHYSICALLY

Bloodshot eyes, lanky hair and spots are all faithfully highlighted by the TV cameras. It's worth trying to get a good night's sleep the night before an interview. Make sure your speaking voice is clear; don't smoke or cough. Having a thick cold is unattractive; to reduce the effect you can sip a glass of warm water before you go on, take a cough drop if needed, but not during the interview!

On both radio and television, voice quality is important.

- Speak as clearly as you can, opening your mouth more widely than usual.

- Breathing properly is essential to good voice production.

- Deeper, lower voices sound better than very high piping ones, so speak in your lowest natural tone.

- Do not try to change your accent; regional accents are very attractive, provided what you say can be clearly understood.

If your mouth unaccountably dries up there are things you can do to get the moisture back: think of squeezing a lemon and sucking in the juice. To add moisture to a dry throat nip the tip of your tongue between your teeth.

OVERCOMING TENSION

You can make yourself appear more relaxed than you are, and even in fact relax yourself a little if you consciously aim to change your state. This can be done in a number of ways.

- Start with the soles of your feet and work upwards, first tensing then relaxing each muscle, all the way up your body to the top of your head.

- If you find your breathing is short, put your hand on your abdomen and concentrate on the in-out movements as you breathe. Try to breathe more deeply (abdominal breathing). Just the activity of focusing on one's breath is relaxing.

- If you only have a second before you start, lift your shoulders towards your ears and drop them sharply a couple of times.

Using body language
In most sports a state of relaxed alertness is the right one for good performance. You must not be too tense or you appear unnatural, nor too laid back or you will miss small cues.

Television viewers can correctly 'read' signs like a tightening round the mouth, or narrowing of the eyes, as tension. Looking over to one side or the other makes you appear slightly untrustworthy. Open, confident smiling enthusiasm and direct eye contact show you know what you are saying and are happy with your role.

BEING PREPARED

The greatest guarantee of achieving clarity is thorough preparation. If you are fully prepared, you know what you are saying and why. You can, if necessary, get the same message over in two or three different ways.

Being prepared means you are not worried about blurting out something you weren't meant to say: integrity and being honest don't necessarily mean revealing all! If you are prepared, you have worked out in advance which of the things you could decide to say are 'green areas' and which should be approached with caution as 'red areas'.

Staying alert yet relaxed
This state is similar to the state achieved in some sports, when you are alert but simultaneously relaxed. Doing a successful interview always has the element of a performance about it. You are alert to every opportunity to get your message over, and relaxed because your purpose is quite clear and you have prepared fully.

CONTROLLING THE INTERVIEW

Surprisingly, to some perhaps, it is not a good idea to 'hold the floor' for as long as possible. Short answers provoke further questions. You stick to your main messages, the interviewer shows their interest, the momentum of the interview speeds up and the viewer becomes absorbed (one hopes) in an interesting conversation.

Encouraging the question you want
The interviewer is aware of the need to maintain a conversational thread, and this is why most follow-up questions are generated by the answers you give. By sticking to your messages, all your answers cover one of your three pre-rehearsed points. If the presenter probes further, you have more opportunity to explain another of your key points.

Remember you will not necessarily be able to give your three messages in your prepared order.

Building bridges
Supposing you have got over two key messages, and the next question doesn't seem to fit well with your third point? This is where there is no substitute for thinking on your feet. You know what your third message is, but you are not quite in a position yet to spout it out. If you did, you'd sound annoyingly like one of those politicians who

arrogantly ignores the question, and says what he was going to say anyway. Viewers have got wise to this quickstep, and they don't like it at all. They see through it, and distrust it. What you have to do is pay attention to the question, answer it rapidly, and then find some way to make a **bridge** or a link between the answer you have just given, and the message you wished to convey. That's fast creative thinking, and you can do it!

Using the two moments in every interview when you can get your message across

You can be sure, in every interview, of just two points where you are bound to have a chance to speak and so get messages over. The first is the first time the interviewer comes to you. Try to make sure you fit the answer well to the question, but move rapidly to one of your messages. Fish out the key message which links best to the question. Make a 'bridge' if need be with the key message.

The second chance (and of course there may be more than two) is when the interviewer is winding up. He or she will indicate by saying something like 'And now finally . . .' or 'we're just running out of time, but can you tell us . . .' Then you know that time is limited, and this is your last opportunity. Use it; under pressure of time you may be forgiven for making a less than clever bridge, but do try to come up with a firm and memorable nutshell, using one or two of the phrases you have worked so hard on.

Grasping other opportunities

There will be other points within an interview when you can insert your key messages:

- An easy question – the interviewer compliments you or your organisation – gives you the chance to bridge quickly on to one of your points.

- A pause allows you to leap in. Remember, do it as if you have just decided to confide in the interviewer.

DOING WELL IN INTERVIEWS

Peter Tidman was personally involved in probably one of the largest media training exercises ever. In his book (see Further Reading) he describes how, at the beginning of the 'Troubles' in Northern Ireland, senior soldiers who were interviewed by broadcast journalists came over to the viewer as very negative. It became Tidman's responsibility to train some 1,000 Army officers in television technique before they left for Ulster.

Tidman played and replayed tapes of their practice interviews and found, to the surprise of some, that rank was no guarantee of good performance. Tidman and his team had a unique opportunity to analyse why some people came over so well in interviews, while others appeared arrogant or uncommunicative. A key point is that the television audience does not know you personally – as in any normal encounter – and so judges you by how you look and by your manner.

Three rules for success

Tidman and his colleagues extracted three rules for successful performance from all the videotapes and analysis.

1. First, you have to attract the audience's attention.
2. Second, you have to keep it, by saying something interesting which involves the audience.
3. Finally, you have to leave behind a message, a lasting impression.

These three simple rules are backed up by some wise advice which is strikingly similar to the method we have come to adopt at Media Minds, although we did not hear of Tidman's work until we were well launched on a similar basis.

Catching their attention

The best way to catch someone's attention is to say 'you!'

which then means 'me'. So if you include a phrase like 'all of you/some of you/many of you/one or two of you/lots of you', you already have their attention. Vicars and priests giving sermons often use the same device.

Bringing in the word 'you' can also distance a speaker from negative connotations. Train companies and water boards are always experiencing a barrage of criticism. One way to deflect it is by shifting the perception: 'Well, when you're running a train company . . .' or 'When you are responsible for making sure that seven million people have water . . .' This obliges the listener to look at things from your point of view.

'We' doesn't work nearly so well: it sounds as if you're trying to take refuge within a group, or even as if you are imitating royalty, as when Margaret Thatcher announced 'We are a grandmother'. There are overtones of aristocracy, distance, arrogance.

Speaking to the individual
The great point about using the second person pronoun is that you seem to speak to everyone individually.

This is why, when asked, we always advise against interrupting the flow of an interviewer's first question by saying 'Good morning'. As far as the audience is concerned, it is of no interest that you have been sitting in a radio car or twiddling your thumbs in a green room and your interview has now started. Instead, get to your point and grab their attention.

Keeping their attention
How do you keep that attention? It is a good idea to have an audience of one in mind as you speak. That one may be, as in my case, my mother-in-law: a highly intelligent woman who was not, however, particularly interested in my special area and knew little about it. If I could make her want to hear more, then that would probably apply to a lot of others as well. An intelligent neighbour or pub companion, even a 12-year-old nephew or niece, might do just as well.

- Never over-estimate their knowledge.

- Never under-estimate their intelligence and shrewdness.

To keep attention, you need to talk in word pictures. What you say needs to engage the mind of the listener. Chapter 5 tells you how to go about creating word pictures. Talking vividly and visually is the best way to maintain the viewer's or listener's attention.

Using examples
Using examples is vital, especially when you want to leave a lasting impression. At a recent literary festival Natasha Spender, wife of the poet, enlivened a session about gardeners and writing by telling how she was out in her Provencal garden at six one morning and heard what she thought was a woodpecker. She stepped quietly down a path until, beyond a hedge, she found the writer John Bayley, tapping away on his typewriter. That served to fix in the memory of her audience her point about how gardens can refresh and inspire writers.

Being conscious of time
Every second counts.

Starting point
Be ready to go straight in to subject matter.

Within the interview
Challenge important inaccuracies.
Recognise the complex, harrying question.
Deal with interruptions by opening up, not complaining.
Don't let them put words in your mouth.
Keep to your agenda.

You the human being
Create rapport.
Be charming.

CASE STUDIES

Carol decides to have media training

In advance of the launch of the company's new set-up in Malaysia later this month, Carol's Communications Director has secured her four interviews on global media, two on different BBC World Service radio programmes, and one each on Sky and CBS News.

Carol will spend a two-hour session with her Comms Director today to identify key messages and then a full morning's Board meeting on the new global communication strategy. Carol is also signed up for a one-day training session with a reputable media training company.

John prepares his Chairman

John has persuaded his Chairman that it is worth going on to a local radio programme to discuss the changes that will be happening as a result of the merger of the two Trusts. The communications strategy is developing well, and internal communications have already started. All staff within the Trust have received full information, in paper form personally to their desks, in team meetings at local level and in site meetings. Consultation has been built into the process. There is no possibility that a member of staff will hear of the plans for the first time from local radio news. Nevertheless, the Chairman has a tendency to reinvent the strategy as he goes along. John has a session with him to agree the three key messages he will be putting over.

John uses the opportunity to remind the Chairman of some of the confidence-building points from his media training, and they run through the video made on that occasion.

Lesley applies yoga to television

Lesley has had two rather bad experiences on television, both on the six o'clock regional news programme. In the first she started coughing uncontrollably, and the interview had to be cut short. In the second, she did not have time to prepare three clear key messages, and felt she had failed to leave any clear impression.

However, she has many of the characteristics of a good TV performer: bright smile, enthusiasm for her subject and a warm, sympathetic appearance. In the middle of her weekly yoga class, Lesley suddenly realises that yoga techniques will be an ideal way for her to achieve the balance she needs between calmness (based on good preparation) and alertness achieved through gentle exercise. Now she always practises yogic breathing before interviews. And they keep on asking her back – Pebble Mill Studios have become quite familiar!

THE INTERVIEW ITSELF – FINAL CHECKLIST

Remember:

- Arrive in plenty of time.

- Be friendly and helpful.

- Check appearance.

- Check notes of key messages and examples.

- Ask whether there has been any change in the line of questioning.

- Ask what the first question will be.

- Make yourself at ease – practise relaxation.

- Have notes with you but do not refer to them during interview.

- Be positive and confident.

- Look alert at all times.

- Look at the interviewer.

- Do not use first names.

- Answer the questions but make sure you get in your key messages.

- Don't let the interviewer re-interpret your answers.

- Stay on the subject.

- Keep it short and simple.

- Use everyday language.

- Refute incorrect or damaging statements.

- Remain calm and courteous.

- Try to have the last word.

John Getgood

7

Making a Success of the Television Interview

What makes a good TV performer? Think of David Bellamy on the environment, Sister Wendy on the arts, Patrick Moore on astronomy, Delia Smith on gastronomy. What they all have in common is boundless enthusiasm for their subject, immense depth of expertise, and the ability to filter highly complex material and present it to a mass audience. Enthusiasm and know-how, you can bring; what about presentation to a mass audience?

On TV, as in any face-to-face encounter, what you say is less important than how you look. A consistent finding of the impact of a person's delivery on an audience shows it is composed of:

7% content
38% voice
55% non-verbal
(Albert Mehrabian)

So 55 per cent of the message is about the way you look. It is only common sense, not vanity, to make use of this fact.

LOOKING GOOD

What can you do to optimise your performance, and make the best possible impression?

- Avoid clothes which are visually 'noisy': loud ties,

finely striped shirts, small checks or busy polyester blends which will 'strobe' on screen.

- Black-and-white does not work well on television, as there is too much reflection from the white.

- Red tends to blotch and bleed.

- Clothes can actually make sounds, leather jackets squeak, some materials rustle, so avoid them if you can.

- Wear clothes you feel happy in but which are perhaps slightly more formal than usual.

- Wear a quiet suit, no flashy jewels or distracting badges.

The eye understands things before the brain, so don't distract from your message. This is not the time to try out a new hairstyle. Dress attractively but conventionally. It's important to be tidy, as you would be for a job interview: no stray hair or smudged mascara; for men – no slipping tie knot and no bit of leg showing between trouser and sock!

Accessories

Glasses or spectacles form a barrier between you and the viewer so, unless you are almost blind without, remove them for the duration of the interview. Light-sensitive glasses can make you look like a member of the Mafia.

Hats are best avoided. When the Director of P & O Ferries was interviewed after the Zeebrugge disaster his rather jaunty tweed fishing hat seemed quite inappropriate.

Using make-up

You will often be offered a little make-up (both men and women), usually a little powder to prevent you glowing under the studio lights. Accept the offer.

If you *prefer* to be made up, do it yourself in advance, just in case the studio does not offer make-up. Men: if you have never practised putting on lipstick, don't try now! Only accept if there is a make-up person to do it for you. In some remote studios, a powder puff and so on may be provided for your own use; best left alone unless you know what you're doing.

Checking your appearance

Without you realising it at the time, the camera may pan over you sitting in the studio, perhaps as the interview is announced in a trailer, or as the interviewer is asking the first question. Hold your tummy in; unbutton your jacket if it's rather tight. Men especially may need to pull their jackets down at the back and sit on them, so that the collar does not stand up awkwardly behind. Practise all this at home in front of a mirror, so that on the day you can give the impression of a restful yet alert person, hands loosely folded, eyes bright and expectant.

Some of this may seem superficial; it is not. You would do the same for a job interview. The point is that television is rather unforgiving and can exaggerate visual discrepancies we hardly notice in real-life encounters.

BEING LIKED AND TRUSTED

Once you're in the studio act as if you're on screen all the time. Be relaxed but avoid looking smug, or as if you're half asleep. Have an open sitting position, with your hands only loosely clasped. People with their arms folded look defensive.

Don't tell lies! Discomfort about what you are saying can show in so many ways. Touching the mouth or face while speaking often indicates anxiety. A long slow blink, where the eyes are partially closed for a moment, can be the sign of someone who is not telling the truth.

Sit still at the end! The camera may be on you as the titles go up, and if you rush away you will give the impression of just having been through an ordeal.

HAVING A CONVERSATION

When you are talking to someone, say at a wedding, you don't keep stopping to smile at the cameraman, do you? It would interfere with any rapport you have built up, it would spoil the conversation. An interview is a kind of conversation. You are talking to the interviewer, and through him or her to the viewer. This is one reason you should always give eye contact to your interviewer.

It is also why you don't say things like 'all the people watching this programme' or 'of course the viewers . . .' There is only one viewer; you are 'sitting in the same room' as them. Your interviewer is, virtually, the viewer too. Through the interviewer, you are speaking to him or her directly. If you achieve rapport and understanding with the interviewer, chances are you have already done so with everyone else.

BEING YOURSELF

Many people going 'on telly' for their company remain in official mode. This is not going to work very well when you are, as it were, sitting in someone's living room. If you behave like a pompous boss, the viewer will want to see you deflated. You have to bring something of yourself into the equation. You are not just Operations Manager or Director of this or that but also a warm human being.

Creating a rapport

As in any important face-to-face encounter, you wish to create *rapport*. Try to think of something you have in common with most of the audience. Make reference to a common experience everyone has had: from finding the toothpaste tube has been squeezed dry to being stalled in traffic. It may seem very artificial, but having one or two 'common humanity' examples up your sleeve is a good idea. Better not to hope to think one up in mid-interview because you could find yourself saying something you

84

didn't quite intend, or drifting away from your agenda and so losing focus.

Funnily enough, it is crucial *not* to mention 'the audience' or even to think of viewers and listeners as a collective group. A more successful approach is to imagine you are in an armchair in someone's sitting room (you virtually are!) and address them as 'you':

- 'What would *you* do if . . .'

- 'How do *you* react to . . .'

- 'What makes *you* feel happy/sad/annoyed . . .' etc

Remember, it is not just the content of what's being said that is conveyed, but your personality. On radio, too, the listener is making judgements about the personality behind the voice.

Try to be your most charming, radiant and friendly self. This may be an interview about your professional role, but what counts is how you seem to be as a person. Whatever is thrown at you, stay calm and remain courteous. If the interviewer becomes heated, you gain sympathy by maintaining an even tone.

USING YOUR VOICE

The sound of your voice accounts for 38 per cent of the impression you make. Think of Bill Clinton's mellow, yet highly intelligent drawl, the Queen's distinctive accent.

Often the sound engineer will ask you what you had for breakfast. In this voice test 99 people out of 100 boringly tell them – and they ask that question several times a day! Why not, instead, say something that will help you and the interviewer to begin on an upbeat note; perhaps practise one of your key messages and give a big smile.

It is vital to speak clearly so that every word is understood. You may have as little as 45 seconds, so a mumble is a complete waste of time.

85

- Project a little more than you normally do.

- Don't talk too fast or too slow.

- Inflection and emphasis add interest.

If you listen to professional newscasters and announcers, you will hear how they vary tone and pitch to keep the listener's interest.

MASTERING THE TECHNIQUES

From your point of view every second counts in an interview, so avoid time-wasters. Don't repeat the question, don't uhm and ah, cut out phrases like 'well to be perfectly honest'.

Getting off to a good start

Sometimes it can seem a bit blunt when the interviewer starts straight off with a question, and many inexperienced interviewees counter by saying 'Good morning Mr Humphrys', or even worse 'Good morning, John' (you have never met him before, he is not a mate, this is a formal situation). Insisting on your right to such pleasantries may make you feel better, but it can irritate the listener, wastes time and may even distract you from making the best response. You could say 'hello' instead, it's shorter, or better still, simply move into your answer. After all, in a news interview, which it would be on the *Today* programme, the content is the significant bit.

If the interviewer has got something wrong, you may have to make a lightning decision about whether to challenge it. If he's called you Mr Brown instead of Mr Smith, you have to correct that, but do it modestly and quickly. If the interviewer has misrepresented you or your company or the situation, then by all means challenge what has been said. But if the error is only tiny, and not significant, it may be better not to break the flow.

Dealing with the complex question

An interviewer trying to unsettle you or to extract an admission may throw two or three questions at you simultaneously. Remain calm and cool, unpick the elements, say something like 'That's really two (or three) different questions; I'll take the one about . . . first.'

Being interrupted

If the interviewer senses you are giving a predetermined policy 'line', you may be interrupted, because s/he thinks you are trying to hide something. There are several other reasons why an interviewer will interrupt:

- Inexperienced interviewees sometimes go on and on talking, as if they are afraid silence will engulf them. A trained interviewer may find they have to 'stop the flow'. A good interview means balanced contributions from both sides.

- If you begin to use a lot of impenetrable jargon, or to use terms not generally understood, the interviewer is bound to interrupt and to 'translate' for the listener.

If you are interrupted, accept there may well be good reason for it and adjust accordingly. Speak with more enthusiasm; keep it simple. Don't start whingeing feebly about being interrupted. Instead, alter your tone slightly, respond helpfully to the interruption, and continue to say precisely what you had planned to say, but with a more open and confiding manner.

Try to give the impression, even when what you are saying is one of your planned key messages, that you are revealing this for the first time, because the interviewer (and, implicitly, the listener) is such an interesting and worthy fellow/person.

If you are interrupted before you have finished your point, it can sound peevish to say 'can I just finish what I was saying, please.' Instead, appeal to the journalist's sense of priorities by saying, 'But, you know, the really significant thing in all this is . . .'

Keeping to your agenda

It is all too easy to answer every question just as if you were under police interrogation, and to forget your own key messages. This is where you have to think quickly, and build a bridge between the question – which you begin to answer in some fashion – and your key point, which you must bring in as soon and as naturally as possible.

You might compliment the interviewer: 'You are quite right to mention that, it's an important point; but even more significant . . .' and then move rapidly to your own key message.

If you use the technique of seeming to reveal something for the first time, in a conversational style which is open and personal, and if you are *interesting*, then the interviewer may well shift on to your ground. But there may still be some pre-planned questions s/he intended to ask, so you may have to use the bridging technique more than once.

Putting words in your mouth

Interviewer to Duncan Fletcher, England cricket coach:

'*Some people might say that if you already have three selectors, and they're not coming up with any decent players, what more can a fourth selector do?*'

Without a challenge to the assumption here, Duncan Fletcher could appear to have admitted that none of his current cricket team is any good. Interviewers will often use the 'some people might say' formula, because it is unchallengeable that 'some people' might say – anything! You may need explicitly to disagree, eg:

'*Every player on the team is there because of what they can offer. What we need is an even bigger pool of excellent players.*'

Watch out for the 'putting words in your mouth' trick where, if you answer yes, you can seem to agree. The soundbite they can use will then present exactly the opposite of the message you wanted to convey.

Doing the interview

Your answers mustn't drone on at great length! If they do, you will never be invited to take part in a live programme again. If it's recorded, your answers will be cut and viewers will not hear what you really said.

Listen carefully to the questions. If a question isn't clear, ask the interviewer to be more specific. Be seen to answer the questions, but work in your own messages too.

Don't fidget with pens or hands, or in your seat.

Your motto should be '**E for easy**'. Use all the Es to remind yourself what's needed:

- **E**arlier the better: to get in the important points

- **E**ssential information only

- **E**ducate your audience: they may not be specialist

- **E**conomise with words – short and pithy please

- **E**asy relaxed manner makes people listen and – most of all –

- **E**njoy it – not many people get the same opportunity!

CLOSING WELL

Ending a panel programme
If you are on a programme where you are part of a panel, it is worth trying to be the person who has the last word. That is more likely to be remembered by the viewer and it can often be a 'summing up' sort of point.

Ending a one-to-one
If the interview is one-to-one, try to fit your final point to the time you sense is available, and make it clear by tone and inflection that you have finished speaking.

You can signal you are ending by concluding the sentence firmly (not with a dying fall, or your final words may be lost). By signalling that you are finishing, you help the interviewer to wind up and so the interview ends on a calm and united note. Both you and the interviewer are aware of each other's timing, and work together to finish the interview satisfactorily.

CASE STUDIES

Carol throws away the pince-nez!

Carol has been invited onto *Business Breakfast*, a fast-moving morning programme aimed at businesspeople, to talk about IT companies in general, and the way mergers and movements of staff are affecting the marketplace for their products. It is quite a complex subject, Carol has a lot to say, and needs to think all the time about the impact of each statement on her own company, Softly, Softly. Fortunately she has brought Peter, one of her PR colleagues, along for company and support. He is an old university friend and they get on very well. Peter can say almost anything to Carol without her taking offence.

The producer has just told Peter that Carol's very trendy spectacles are catching the studio lights in an unfortunate way, and asks Peter if Carol is very short-sighted or if she could manage without wearing her specs. Peter has also noticed that Carol is wearing a permanent frown, because she is concentrating so hard.

Peter waits until they are alone in the green room, then suggests to Carol she needs to lighten up a little to get her full, bright and bubbly personality across. The glasses are detracting from that, he says, and so is what he calls her 'frozen perma-frown'. Carol responds with peals of laughter, removes the spectacles and consciously relaxes the muscles round her eyes.

As a result, she comes over much more 'like herself' and the interview is a success.

John is a person with friends, too

John has had a very difficult year. The merger of the two
Trusts has been traumatic, with many staff having to find
new jobs. John sometimes feels very tired of defending the
Health Service. Now the Chairman has decided John
should do a very testing interview on the *Nine o'Clock
News*, following the outbreak of an infection in three of the
wards at St Erwin's Hospital.

Last night John went for a drink with an old
schoolfriend, who told him how the outbreak had affected
his mother, who was in for a straightforward hip operation.
In discussion with the Chairman John decides to refer
indirectly and fleetingly to his friend's mother, who is also
someone he has known well all his life. They decide he will
work into the interview something of his own reaction to
hearing about the effects on his friend's mother, as a way
of bridging to one of the core messages: the Trust's
sympathy and care for members of the community using its
hospitals.

Lesley spends money on her voice

Lesley comes from Birmingham and has a very strong
regional accent. Ben, one of the press team from
headquarters, comes down to listen to her practice tape
and advise on preparation for a TV phone-in programme
she is doing in a couple of week's time.

Ben is very congratulatory about the way Lesley handles
all the content issues; he notices that the timbre and tone
of her voice are excellent. Unfortunately, her 'Brummie'
speech is a little sloppy, so that her accent seems to
interfere with the full understanding of what she is
saying.

Regional accents are perfectly acceptable, and can be
warm and friendly. The only problem here is the way
Lesley enunciates and projects her voice. With
considerable tact, and a couple of well chosen anecdotes
about well known presenters who benefited from voice
training, Ben is able to persuade Lesley to take a short,
professional voice production course.

Lesley is secretly rather pleased that headquarters thinks it worthwhile spending so much money on her!

ACTION POINTS

1. The way you look and sound are at least as important as what you say.

2. The viewer is curious about you as a person. Be liked and trusted, speak clearly and above all, be yourself – or yourself at your best!

3. Consciously start to develop and master the techniques to start and close well, to deal with interruptions and to avoid having words put in your mouth.

8

Doing Different Kinds of Interview

We all tend to carry in our heads a prototype of the media interview. Ideally, you and the interviewer are both sitting in an armchair, perhaps with a nice comforting table in front. The camera flatters you and there is plenty of time to work up a good deal of rapport with the interviewer.

But what if the interviewer in a radio studio is wearing headphones, and doesn't seem to be listening to you? Or the television studio is large and bare, your presenter is three metres away, and he's looking at his own notes and giving the distinct impression you are not to say a word until he's ready? What if you cannot see the interviewer at all because you're in a remote studio, and he's in London? Or you're in a radio car, or even perhaps sitting in your bedroom early in the morning, waiting for a call? Increasingly, cost savings in broadcasting organisations and the speed of news events mean that interviews are carried out under all sort of conditions, not always most comfortable to you.

Knowing:

- what to expect
- and how to get the best out of each context

can help you give your best performance, even in unpromising circumstances. And remember before the interview that *they* need *you*.

Make sure you are as comfortable and relaxed as it is possible to be. This is likely to be more effective than complaining afterwards.

DOING A RADIO INTERVIEW BY TELEPHONE

Doing an interview down the telephone line has drawbacks:

- the sound quality may be so poor that they decide to drop the interview.
- You have no eye contact with the interviewer, so rapport is reduced.

On the other hand it's likely to be live, so if you are *sure* of your main points you can get them over succinctly and without editing.

Making an assessment
Ask why it's being done on the telephone. Do they assume you don't have time to come into the studio? Is the studio too far away?

If you can make time you may be more comfortable in a studio, with some chance of talking to the interviewer beforehand and finding out more about the programme. You will be geared up, alert and prepared.

The trouble with a telephone call from your office in the middle of the day is that *you* may not be well focused, and so may not perform at your best.

DOING A RADIO PHONE-IN

If you are the resident expert, then you have been asked to take part in the phone-in because of who you are and what you know. Preparation is needed, not really to cover the subject matter but for the paraphernalia and techniques of this kind of radio.

You will be given earphones, and probably a pencil and pad. Use the pencil to note each caller's name – only too easy to forget, when you cannot see them.

Being the expert

As the acknowledged expert, you really have nothing to prove, you can be relaxed and pleasant. Rather than short, snappy answers, you can develop themes and notions. You don't have to project yourself, more try to bring interesting points out of the conversation, and entertain the listener. No harm in flattering your questioners, putting them at their ease, drawing them out.

You should be given the full name of the caller just before they speak. Jot down the name, and sound friendly by starting 'Hello Mrs Brown . . .' (or however they've introduced themselves).

If you need time to think before giving an answer, ask the caller a factual question. This increases your knowledge of their dilemma, or their point of view if it is an opinion piece.

As phone-in 'expert' you can sound gentler, be less of a performer. Talk in calm, measured tones; make your voice warm and friendly.

THE PRE-RECORDED, TAPED RADIO INTERVIEW

When a journalist comes to you with a tape recorder you have plenty of opportunity to ask questions and get a clear idea of the nature of the programme.

Above all, you have an excellent chance to get to know the interviewer, and to form a relationship which you may want to maintain for the future:

- Find something you have in common with them; show that you understand their job, the pressures they are working under.

- Help them to do the best possible, the most professional and entertaining interview you can achieve together.

- Offer to supply further information if required.

The great danger lies in saying too much and talking for too long. If you do this, you hand over to the journalist the power to decide what are the more interesting parts of the conversation, and perhaps letting them edit out just those things you most wanted to say.

Being clear

Prepare your main points – and your illustrations and anecdotes.

When you have said what you meant to say, stop.

If it doesn't go quite right, you can ask them to start again. However, *they* will decide, back in the editing room, which version sounds better. If you want to be sure they don't use the earlier version, say 'Actually, that was wrong' or 'That isn't quite true' or 'I made a mistake there'.

THE STUDIO RADIO INTERVIEW

Try to arrive early; it may give you useful time to talk to the producer and interviewer before going on air. On the other hand don't count on this, you may literally have only a couple of minutes while the last record plays out.

Usually there is a red light visible when the programme is on air. In a radio studio it is easy to forget how faithfully the microphone will pick up every sound. Don't rustle papers, shift around too much in your seat, or move the microphone once you've started.

- Remember how much time you've got.

- Ensure you get your main points over.

- Stop altogether when you've said what you want to say.

- Let your voice indicate you're coming to an end (but not a dying fall, or your words will fade away!)

Smile even though you're invisible. People can 'hear' a smile.

Be alert for the unexpected!

DOING A FACE-TO-FACE INTERVIEW IN A TV STUDIO

If you are in the studio with a presenter, look directly at the person who is interviewing you. Leave it to the camera operator to find the right angle.

If it's in the main news studio you may not meet the presenter until you get there. He or she will have been briefed by the researcher who spoke to you beforehand, and probably also by the producer. It can be difficult to establish any kind of rapport, as they may be absorbed in switching to your subject, which they may consider for only three minutes before moving to another.

Live and recorded interviews

A studio interview may be live or recorded. If recorded it can be edited later, and this is helpful if they need to remove your 'uhms' and 'ahs'. In a live interview you obviously have more control over what is broadcast, but this is only much use if you are confident you can speak fluently, without pauses. If in fact you're a bit long-winded, with a tendency to use jargon or hesitate a lot, they will not risk another live interview, and may never ask you back at all. In this case, pre-recorded interviews can be like touched up photographs: they improve your performance!

There are many different contexts: you may be tape recorded in your office, interviewed from a radio car or in a public place, taken out of a meeting for a quick comment.

THE PANEL INTERVIEW

The big danger in being part of a panel set-up is that your speaking time is reduced because the others do all the talking.

There are at least four points in this scenario where you can get over your main messages:

- The first question. The interviewer can be counted on to bring you in at least once. Answer the question, but move swiftly on to your key points.

- A pause of more than five seconds. Gives you leeway to dive in but be succinct, and if possible, amusing.

- Any question or point where you can make a bridge to your messages. Stay alert, look for the opportunity, much as you might in a real life conversation, for instance at a dinner party where your boss was present.

- The last question. Interviewers and presenters always give a signal for the final question. They will say 'Now, we're running out of time . . .' or 'Could you say, in one minute, please . . .' It's your last and possibly even your best chance!

BEING INTERVIEWED FOR TV 'DOWN THE LINE'

The interview may be in a remote studio – down the line via a fixed camera, in a room not much bigger than a broom cupboard.

Ask beforehand for the name of the person on-site who will help you make contact with the programme and interviewer. If you don't they may assume you know the ropes, and leave you to connect up and switch on.

Assuming you are given help, you will be miked up so that your voice is heard, and have an earpiece through which you listen to the interviewer. This can be a little unnerving, as you will not be able to see who you are speaking to (though *they* can see *you*). The only visual clue you will have is the shot of yourself; it's probably best not to keep looking at that.

Looking lively

Down-the-line interviews are the *only* time you should look directly at the camera. Indeed if you don't look into the camera, your eyes will move from side to side and you will appear decidedly shifty. It can help to imagine the person you're speaking to at the bottom of the lens, as it were. Smile brightly at them, use lots of expression, as you would if there was a person there. The great danger with remote interviews is that you begin to look wooden and lifeless, because you have no one to respond to.

DOING AN OUTSIDE BROADCAST

A film crew may arrive at your office to record an interview. They will choose a location with suitable lighting or which can be lit by cameras.

- Then they will record 'noddies' and 'cutaways' to use in editing.

- They will want 'set up' shots of you at work.

- They will need film of your building, or your operation, the vans in the car park, the ducks in the pond etc to go with the commentary.

Be ready for the possibility that they will want to go outside, or to the canteen or factory floor in search of background atmosphere. Sometimes a producer may choose a completely different location – they may put a tennis ball manufacturer at Wimbledon, a computer programmer in a school etc.

Considering location

If you have a good location idea yourself, the producer may buy it. Farmers, gardeners and other outdoor people look completely different, and much better, out of doors. Alfresco interviews can create a powerfully positive feel. For instance, Tony Blair was interviewed in the rose garden at Number 10 Downing Street, with fuchsias in full flower behind him, after the breakdown of the Irish peace process in the summer of 1999. The beauty and associations of the surroundings outweighed the rather negative elements of the news story.

On the other hand, you can look like a drowned rat if they interview you in the rain and don't provide an umbrella. This is where having a PR person to accompany you is helpful, they will not let you be sucked into looking foolish or at a disadvantage.

Be careful where they film you. Don't forget, the background is part of the picture too. Apparently, when there are books behind a speaker he or she comes over as more respected and authoritative. An editorial decision has already been made to interview you, you are needed, so don't be afraid to make a fuss if you are really unhappy about something.

BEING 'DOORSTEPPED'

Usually following an emergency or in a crisis situation of some kind (see Chapter 9), you may well be caught off guard by finding a reporter, complete with microphone and cameraman, outside your office, in the airport as you arrive from somewhere or even outside your own front door as you depart in the morning.

- Rule number one is do not move away or otherwise try to hide.

There is a telling piece of film of a government minister marching rapidly through a series of doors in some hospital, being pursued by a reporter and cameraman. What the Minister said was probably fine, but the overwhelming visual message was that he appeared to be running away from the cameras.

CHOOSING LIVE OR RECORDED

If you are a first-time interviewee, you may appreciate the assurance that if you fudge your lines they will re-record and let you have another go. However, the very possibility of re-doing the interview means you may not give your best performance. And of course a pre-recorded interview can be edited in a way you might not be pleased with.

Professional ethics will not permit complete distortion. The ITC Programme Code (and the BBC's is similar) says:

> Editing to shorten recorded interviews must not distort or misrepresent the known views of the interviewee.

If you still prefer pre-recorded, the best course is to say what you want to say, and stop as soon as your messages have been conveyed. This means you must be sure to have picked out your priority message and got that one over at all costs.

As you gain confidence in interviews, you will begin to prefer to go live. Spontaneity and freshness will be retained, and no one can alter your words or cut out what you thought was a vital message. However, if a bigger story comes along, and your live interview doesn't fit the time space anymore, you may find it is dropped.

HANDLING THE HOSTILE INTERVIEW

On some occasions the interviewer is almost professionally required to be hostile: you are a company that has just withdrawn food from its shelves because it has been tampered with; you are the chairman of a bus company and your buses have been proved to be defective, one in an accident causing loss of life, etc etc.

The interviewer begins by saying 'How can (your company) possibly justify this?' or 'How could you allow this to happen?'

Clearly, you must be most thoroughly prepared for such an interview. What can you do to reduce the hostility, which is also probably present in the minds of many viewers/listeners?

- Acknowledge and accept what you can and must.

- Empathise with whoever is suffering.

- Move strongly and convincingly on to what you/your company are now doing to remedy things.

CASE STUDIES

Carol is glad she spared the time

Carol is asked to give an interview on a popular morning discussion programme. They offer her the choice of coming over to the studio in London, or speaking on a specially set up phone line. Carol calculates that she will 'lose' an hour-and-a-half from her day if she goes over to the studios, but decides the interview is worth it.

When she arrives, two hours later, she finds they have invited in a rival firm to make another comment, and the item is now going to be 95 seconds longer than originally envisaged.

In the green room, Carol has a chat with her colleague from another company. They agree they do not want to be in competition with one another, and also agree what different things they can say.

As the topic is one of genuine news interest there is lots to say, and the moment of co-operation in the green room pays off, for both Carol and her 'rival' perform well.

John looks for the right background

John has a very difficult interview coming up. Eleven elderly patients have died of flu in one hospital in one week. There are reasons, and there is reassurance he can give, but John has recognised this is one interview which could turn out very hostile.

He draws in a photogenic doctor and a nurse. He also agrees with the programme's producer beforehand to have a location shot in one of the hospital's wards. Before the team arrives, John works out a suitably attractive backdrop and arranges a fresh vase of flowers strategically in the background. The interview goes 'as well as can be expected'.

Lesley finds she likes 'down the line'

Lesley has done so many interviews that she is becoming quite well known at her regional radio studio. On the sixth occasion she comes in to do a 'down the line' the reception staff don't even bother to take her down to the studio. They just hand her the key, knowing she can switch on and make contact with London.

Lesley likes radio interviews down the line because, after her voice production class, she knows she is speaking well and clearly, and being alone in a remote studio she can even act a little bit. She sounds enthusiastic and relaxed, and keeps being invited back because she sounds so 'natural'!

ACTION POINTS

1. What are the main things to remember for a phone-in programme where you are the resident expert?

2. What are the pros and cons of an outside broadcast as against a studio interview?

3. Is it better to be interviewed live or pre-recorded?

9

Talking to the Media in a Crisis

KNOWING IT'S A CRISIS

How do you know you are in the middle of a crisis? The main elements are:

- surprise

- increased 'noise'

- lack of real information.

There will be a feeling of being under extreme time pressure and at the same time exposed to the world outside. In a crisis you may well be dealing with familiar issues, but without the usual amount of time to think and plan. An outside agenda is driving you. The world external to your company has somehow delivered an unexpected input or signal. It may not be until a news room calls you for a comment that you realise the crisis has started. You are carrying out management 'in a goldfish bowl', that is, in the public domain.

Thames Trains knew at 8.19 on the morning of 5 October 1999 that they had a crisis (day of the Paddington rail crash).

- A crisis is a moment of dissonance.
- A crisis is anything that appears in any newspaper three or four times in one day.

Typical crisis situations can arise from health risks, unexpected deaths, testing, product recall, abuse of some kind: one of your products presents a danger to the public; a life-threatening incident happens on your premises; an employee reveals something potentially damaging.

Planning for a crisis

Proper risk-assessment would have thrown up each of these as a future possibility, though the reality will often differ in some key respect. The point is, it's possible to plan ahead for the worst scenario in each of these categories:

- What is the worst damage one of your products could do?

- What accident or environmental incident could conceivably apply to your area?

- What is the most difficult and damaging thing an employee could say about your concern?

You might argue that an aeroplane falling out of the sky onto your building is impossible to plan for, yet two well known incidents of this kind were in fact magnificently handled.

When an aircraft crashed onto a piece of motorway near Kegworth, the British Midlands spokesperson was on the spot at an early point, and gave press interviews immediately.

When the Pan Am jet fell out of the sky onto Lockerbie, the police cordoned off the area and painstakingly collected necessary evidence; the local community rose to the occasion too with an essentially human response.

The common elements in both cases were:

- behaving well – even heroically – under pressure

- having good procedures to follow

- and keeping up the flow of communication.

Being doorstepped in a crisis

How do you react if the first you know of the crisis is a journalist informing you as you enter your building in the morning?

1. Quickly find out from them what has happened, off camera.

2. Listen carefully to what they have to say – they are already formulating the storyline.

3. Escort them to a secure area, ask them to wait.

4. Get your response ready, gathering any available information.

5. If you can assemble your thoughts and come up with a short message satisfying all the requirements of a good crisis interview (see below), agree to be interviewed.

6. If you cannot, make your refusal politely. Only do so if you know you will lose more than you gain by a TV appearance. Do not refuse to comment, instead try to fix an interview time for later in the day.

RISK-ASSESSMENT: THE BRAINSTORMERS

An internal group, containing at least some senior management personnel, needs to meet periodically, perhaps once a year or once every six months, to brainstorm about all the possible crises that could hit. After the first time this may mean revising the previous list. New products, new partnerships, any change in strategy, all have the potential to produce a different sort of crisis.

Brainstorming should be a free-flowing, creative sort of exercise. You need to make sure that every idea the group generates is recorded. The 'yes, but' kind of intervention should be banned, if you want to get a comprehensive list. A senior manager saying 'yes, but that could never happen because . . .' will only stymie debate and limit imagination. 'Yes, and . . . ?' is a more appropriate comment.

Brainstormers' questions
The brainstormers need to ask: What crises could hit us?

The operation
Many products carry predictable risks; a chemical company and a hospital will already have thought through the well known risks. Supermarkets know that sabotage of controversial products is possible. Risk exposure, eg chemicals, machinery, health, environment, sabotage, is something every enterprise needs to consider periodically.

   Government action can provoke a crisis, if you have not foreseen how new legislation or changed policy can affect you.

Your employees
Chronic stress and low morale can produce disgruntled employees who want to get back at the employer. The quality of your staff and the way they are expected to deal with mini crises can all contribute to the likelihood or otherwise of a major crisis. If output has been rushed for some reason, or the management ethos is 'them and us', if major staff changes have led to multiple redundancies, if rumours abound about restructuring, then the ground is ripe for disaffection.

Customer complaints
These are a good guide to sensitive areas where you need to be alert for negative occurrences.

THE CRISIS TEAM

The brainstormers need not be the same people as the crisis team. A small team of key managers must be

prepared and trained to react rapidly in a crisis, so that
they are in a position to recognise, define and deal with the
issues and problems that arise. They should come together
at least every six months for the following purposes:

- Review crisis procedures and the crisis manual if you
  have one.
- Remind themselves of the resources and facilities
  they can call on.
- Add or subtract members from the group in the light
  of personnel changes.

The team's role
The crisis team needs to cover the main functions of the
organisation and include senior people who have the
authority to speak for the organisation as a whole. Decide
who will form the crisis team, review on an annual basis.
When the crisis occurs, they need to be relieved from
normal day-to-day work as long as the crisis lasts, and they
have a number of tasks to perform:

- Defining the problem and assessing its short- medium-
  and long-term impact.

- Keeping communications flowing:
  —centralising, filing and keeping abreast of
  communications in and out
  —remembering all the groups who have to be kept
  informed
  —dealing with the media; preparing and delivering
  clear consistent messages for as long as the crisis lasts.

- Ensuring that the business continues to be managed
  effectively.

Defining and assessing the problem
- Clarify what the immediate problems are.

- Assess the longer-term impacts.

- Look at the worst things that could happen.

- Keep the short- and long-term scenarios in mind all the time and do not forget the important longer-term.

KEEPING THE COMMUNICATIONS FLOWING

Keeping abreast of communications in and out
The team needs a room, telephones, communication centre. There must be a central focus for the information coming in and going out.

For any crisis, ask:

- Who are the audiences? What do they want to hear? How can we satisfy their needs for information and for reassurance about our humanity, credibility and competence? (Your own employees are always one of the audiences you need to keep in touch with.)

- What media of communication will we use – press release/ press statement/direct communication of various kinds/ spokesperson to different audiences?

- What are we going to say? What are the messages? Are they consistent with our core key messages for normal times?

Remembering the groups who have to be kept informed

1. Understand the media's agenda, and find answers to their obvious questions.

2. If you really don't know the answer, describe vigorously what you are doing to find out.

3. Have information flowing in and out through a central point.

4. Use a checklist of all internal and external groups who need to be kept informed.

Inside groups: employees and their families

- managers at all levels
- headquarters
- the salesforce
- trade unions or works representatives
- front-line staff on switchboard, security, reception

Outside groups: customers and suppliers

- industry associations
- industry experts and commentators (who might be invited in by the media)
- residents and local community leaders
- politicians
- technical experts and specialists
- local authorities
- regional and national government

The media are the most important outside group, because communications are key in a crisis. You will be in a strong position if you can view the media as your allies.

Clamming up

The most common reaction is to try to buy time to plan a statement, consult the lawyers, speak to the chairman, while saying nothing publicly. Your management group may come up with lots of good reasons why you should keep quiet at the moment:

— The chief executive: 'We need to get all the facts first' (all the facts will not be available for some time if ever!).
— The lawyers: 'We can't risk the legal implications/we can't admit responsibility/we must be very careful . . .'

— The production director: 'We might reveal proprietary information.'

— Even the communications director: 'We don't have a spokesperson.'

But to say nothing at all may prove disastrous. It can end in the dreaded report 'X declined to comment', leaving the public to conclude no smoke without fire/they're hiding something/guilty!

If you say there is no one available to speak, the journalists will merely talk to someone in the emergency services, neighbouring businesses, industry experts, pressure groups, the local press, the specialist press.

HANDLING A CRISIS WELL

Several years ago, when tests indicated that there just might be a problem with Perrier water, Perrier's pragmatic management instantly withdrew every bottle on the market and warned the public. At some considerable cost they took out one million bottles. In fact the risk was very small indeed. The prompt action convinced everyone that Perrier really cared about quality. The marketing effort which followed was also fine: Perrier continues to this day to be a successful company.

Compare that series of reactions with the British Government debacle over BSE and 'mad cow disease'. As early as 1987, James Ehrlichman suggested in *The Guardian* a possible link between CJD and BSE, and this danger has been in and out of the public domain ever since.

Fear of the media is understandable, but you can analyse what they want:

• to hunt down a good story

• to find out the root cause

• to seek to attribute blame

111

and you can respond positively. How do you say and do
the right thing, while avoiding obvious pitfalls like
unnecessarily admitting liability?'

Addressing the emotions

Present a human face. While your spokesperson should of
course remain calm, too much of a stiff upper lip can seem
to say you don't care. When something bad has happened,
someone has usually been hurt. Acknowledge that by
showing that you *feel* their pain. Use feeling words, not just
'of course we have sympathy with the relatives' but
something more simple and true to the feelings you are
able to tap in yourself.

Your spokesperson must be able to speak with
humanity, to present a human face. In a health context, a
doctor or nurse with senior management responsibility is a
better choice of spokesperson than a besuited bureaucrat.
But personality is more important than role.

Understanding and sharing the concerns

Something has gone wrong. You can say 'this should not
have happened' or 'something has clearly gone wrong, and
we want to know why' without making the lawyers jump
up and down.

You also need to give reassurance. At the start, that may
be just a report on what you are now doing, and a promise
to speak again – within the hour if necessary.

Demonstrating commitment to act

Say what you are doing, what you have already done, what
you are about to do. Use active verbs. Show that you are
committed.

At this point you can also try to introduce some
perspective.

Following the golden rule

The most golden rule with all crisis communication is:

- tell the truth.

112

After the Paddington rail crash of 1999, the crisis team was so concerned to demonstrate their honesty that they phoned every press room to correct an earlier statement about the amount of training the driver of the crashed train had had. As a result there were no stories along the lines of 'Rail company misled the public on driver training and experience'.

KNOWING WHAT MAKES GOOD CRISIS HANDLING

Now the crisis is upon you. What must you do?

- Have a plan; stick to it but be flexible.

- Keep the crisis team happy.

- Keep the employees happy.

- Keep the public happy.

Telling them what they need to hear

A sound principle of the psychology of communicating in a crisis is that you should base what you say *on what the public need to hear*, rather on what you would like to tell them.

What did the public want to hear in the wake of the Paddington rail crash?

— that everything is being done to save lives and reduce the effect of injury
— that relatives are being kept informed and humanely dealt with
— that those responsible will admit responsibility and not deny it
— that all those concerned – the rail companies, the police, the emergency services – are behaving semi-heroically and with human warmth.

It is the appearance of the top person which will be key, and his or her attitude and body language as well as the actual words need to convey sympathy, concern, reassurance and competence.

Communicating effectively
In a crisis you are speaking to those:

- who are affected by the crisis
- who can affect us
- who are involved in the crisis
- who need to know

How do we communicate with them?
For example do you know how to set up a telephone hotline? Perhaps you need to appoint a supplier now.

What other resources and facilities do we need?
- venue: dedicated facilities; alternative venue
- controlled entry
- adequate room, furniture, flip charts etc
- a number of telephones, one with an ex-directory outgoing line
- hotline facility
- mobile communicators and cellphones
- fax, e-mail, internet
- TV/radio studio facilities to rehearse interviews
- TV and radio monitoring equipment plus, eg, Reuters
- ISDN line for video-conferencing
- stationery
- access to mass mailing
- a means of logging all actions

- services, eg press/broadcast monitoring, printing, distribution etc
- if feasible a means of recording telephone conversations
- nearby or on-site sleeping facilities
- refreshments
- separate and nearby venue for hosting the press.

What are the messages?
Try to identify a number of core messages, eg:

1. Feeling – the human face: sorry, or if you can't say that then regret, sympathy, concern, compassion. Show that you care.
2. Reassurance – how you will put it right, make amends, ensure it doesn't happen again.
3. Competence – what you are doing about it.

What training do we need?
Crisis media training is not the same as crisis training, it is only part of it. But media training is essential, people behave completely differently under skilful questioning.
  Check out media trainers by:

- asking to speak to some of the companies they have trained
- checking their credentials as professional trainers
- looking for trainers who understand something about communication psychology
- seeing if they understand what it is like to be on your side of the fence.

You also need to:

- understand the nature of crisis and the psychology involved

- have practice at simulations as a team
- know what your crisis procedures are.

Contents of crisis manual/procedure

1. Introduction. Description of what is expected of team members, corporate philosophy, how to use the manual.

2. Brief summary of company's procedures.

3. Crisis team. Names, responsibilities, 24-hour contact numbers, stand-ins if ill.

4. Audiences. List, emergency numbers for employee communications, lawyers etc.

5. Messages. Reminder list.

6. Resources. Location of crisis room, how to operate communications modes etc.

7. Media reminder checklists on handling the media and preparing for and succeeding with interviews.

8. Background briefs on the company.

GIVING PRESS CONFERENCES IN A CRISIS

A press conference is a key strategic opportunity – but *only* if you know why you're holding one!

Your own press conference is your opportunity to 'shop window' the organisation to the media. You can put your best face forward, you have the chance to set the agenda. Yet even the best-managed press conferences are rarely trouble-free. An unexpected question from an intelligent commentator can pierce to the heart of unresolved organisational ambiguities.

The most common sources of difficulty are:

1. roles of the spokespeople

2. lack of consistency between media messages and the organisation's strategic objectives.

Preparations

This is just as desirable for a press conference as for any other major strategic business meeting. Find out who will be there, what media they represent. Think how you will fill the gaps if key players do not attend. Be aware of different newspapers' 'angles' and the audience behind each medium or publication. Through the press conference you are speaking indirectly to some of your most important clients or stakeholders.

So prepare just as for a high-profile media interview. Rehearse the whole event if you can.

Get your act together!

Even the announcement . . . was surrounded by disorder. The press conference was announced and postponed without explanation. Insiders revealed yesterday that confusion arose because of a 'major row' between Ms McIntosh and Vivien Duffield, who chairs the Royal Opera House Trust.

. . . There were disagreements, too, with Lord Chadlington . . . The animus was evident during the new season press conference, when it was eventually held. 'Lord Chadlington repeatedly interrupted her and dealt with her in a generally patronising manner' said one observer . . .

Independent, 14 May 1997, reporting on departure of Genista McIntosh, Chief Executive of the Royal Opera House

---

If there are differences of opinion between prominent members of the senior management team, then be sure, they will come to light in a press conference. It is essential to have the fullest accord and agreement amongst board members in advance of speaking to the media. Without that accord, it is difficult if not impossible to convey a clear public message. Your time and effort may not just be wasted, the press conference can be counterproductive, even fatal to one or more members of the team, as in the above example.

If more than one board member is there, you need to decide who is going to speak on what. Both of you trying to reply to the same question can look disorganised, or even imply competition between you.

Who speaks?

Be quite clear who is there, who speaks and why.

Expect that after a press conference journalists will seek one-to-one interviews with anyone who has been presenting at the press conference. They may choose a junior researcher or someone other than the chairman, because they think this could produce a new or more interesting angle.

You need to have thought through beforehand, as a board or senior management team, whether you are happy for *anyone* who has spoken for you at the press conference to undertake an interview like this.

If your junior person has not received media training, and is not fully aware of the organisation's policy on key matters – and, particularly, sensitive matters – you need to think through your attitude. If someone in this position can only speak 'under supervision' of a more senior manager, then it may be better not to field them as an interviewee at all.

On the other hand, if your organisation is a very open one, and you allow large numbers of employees to speak on your behalf, then you can broaden the base of those presenting at press conferences.

What you cannot easily do is allow someone to speak for

the organisation in the 'presenting' part of the conference and then refuse, on their behalf, a one-to-one interview.

Spin-offs from a press conference

If you regularly hold press conferences you may find the same journalists and broadcasters turning up to cover your story. They are the expert for that journal on your sector or on you as an organisation. It is therefore very important to make these people your friends. They can be allies in the sense that they do actually understand what you are about and are therefore less likely to make gross mistakes in reporting what you are doing.

On the other hand, they are necessarily sharp observers, and will note any departure from previous policy, or shift in emphasis from statements you have made before.

Checklist of questions

1. Have you done a risk assessment of your operation?

2. Have you chosen a risk team?

3. Do you have a procedural plan?

4. Do you know which audiences you will need to speak to?

CASE STUDIES

Carol's crisis at Softly, Softly

A piece of software produced by Carol's company is disastrously reported as corrupting date and time systems on computers. In fact the report is untrue.

Carol's crisis team explains to the media that it is urgently investigating the report, and promises that if customers have suffered losses, Softly, Softly will repay them.

Within hours the report is found to have started in a

share dealing room where there were other, unconnected problems. Those responsible unreservedly apologise, and clear Carol's company. Softly, Softly's prompt public statement, and its apparently generous promise, are remembered within the industry for some time and enhance its reputation.

John and the ambulanceman's sandwich
John's hospital faces crises every month – in the casualty ward, every day. Their procedures are well honed, and every member of each team understands what they are expected to do in a crisis. Even so, every week brings a new twist or a story with another angle. This week it is the ambulancemen and their sandwiches. One ambulance was late for a call because the driver had gone to get a sandwich. As a result, all ambulances are issued with an emergency ration to be used when time does not permit a sandwich stop!

Lesley goes on another course
Lesley's charity helps families in crisis, and is used to situations where desperate remedies have to be sought. She has just been promoted to head the Birmingham office. The new element for Lesley now is the need to explain everything to the media. She is going up to headquarters in London for a special briefing on emergency and crisis procedures.

ACTION POINTS

1. What is the best way to assess the risks your enterprise may face?

2. Can you make a list of the 'inside groups' and 'outside groups' that would apply to your situation in a crisis?

3. What are the three things you need to communicate in a crisis?

THE PRESS CONFERENCE – FINAL CHECKLIST

Remember:

- Press conferences are not for trivial announcements.
- Choose location for convenience and impact.
- Make sure it will be well attended.
- Rehearse.
- Prepare major statements in advance.
- Prepare press release.
- Time press conference to meet relevant deadlines.
- Select panel carefully.
- Lay out room with space for television cameras.
- Decide on strategy for media interviews: who, when?
- Start with introduction and schedule from press officer.
- Introduce main speakers – give them status.
- Take questions from the floor for pre-arranged time.
- Make sure journalists identify themselves.
- Choose appropriate location for one-to-one interviews.

John Getgood

10

Knowing When to Talk to the Media

KNOWING WHY YOU WANT TO TALK TO THE MEDIA

The first question to ask yourself before you accept an invitation to go on TV or radio is:

- 'What is my purpose in doing this?'

What do you want to achieve? Are you trying to promote your book, or to kill a negative story which could harm the company you work for? Is it a good opportunity to put over the general positive messages that your advertising and PR are geared to?

If you don't know what you hope to get out of it, then stop and think a bit (see Chapter 4).

The second question to ask is:

- 'Do I really know my stuff?'

A media interview is pretty testing: a good journalist will tax you with the most difficult and searching questions they can devise – and you are expected to know the answers. Knowing about your company in a generalised way is not enough. You also need key statistics which trip off your tongue pretty easily, and are absolutely accurate: how many widgets you produce, how many people or machines it takes, how long you have been in business. If you have answers – accurate and well grounded – to all the major questions which can be legitimately asked, you are only just as competent as someone facing a journalist needs to be.

Being prepared

If you know *why* you want to go on radio or television, and if you have at your fingertips all the necessary facts, you can go ahead, but preparation will still of course be necessary and media training may be desirable.

Media training used to be the preserve of the elite few – senior politicians, top-flight chairmen or chief executives in sensitive positions learned through hard experience that arguing your case in front of the camera does not always come naturally. Nowadays every organisation, large or small, sooner or later finds itself the object of media attention, and even quite middle-ranking managers may be fielded on local radio or television.

This should not be something to dread, but an opportunity to grasp with two hands – assuming you are well prepared for it. The most important benefit is that your good points and strengths are suddenly revealed to a much wider public. Everybody has the option to get the best out of the media spotlight.

SELLING THE COMPANY

Ideally an organisation's communication strategy includes – along with clear messages to distinct audiences – the conscious aim of positive media coverage. Media interest is very hard to obtain normally; when it does arise, it is good to be in a position to recognise the opportunity and make the most of it. Through the media you can reach into the minds of thousands, even millions of people including those who need to understand your key messages: potential customers, your stakeholders, those you want to influence.

Safeguarding your company

By being prepared you can also be in a position to safeguard your company from the adverse effects of possibly bad publicity. If you doubt this, listen to a few news interviews where the story appears to be very negative for one side or the other. A good spokesperson can quickly reverse or neutralise apparently negative messages, and replace them with the more positive view he or she holds. Much depends on the quality of the arguments and the thought behind them. Even more, as we know, depends on the impression made by the individual spokesperson, and whether he or she displays honesty, integrity and grace under fire.

HELPING YOUR OWN CAREER

Spokespeople who acquit themselves well may be seen as a saviour by the organisation, and even begin to build a more successful career for themselves. The NATO spokesman Jamie O'Shea, for example, sweated many times under the lights and the sharp questioning of the world's journalists. His consistency and frankness, as well as his own warmth and humanity, endeared him to many. Despite the difficult messages he often had to convey, he himself became an extremely well known and well liked figure, virtually indispensable in his role. If you are good at it, being a spokesperson may enhance your own career and prospects, as many people who did not originally set out to be professional communicators have discovered.

MAINTAINING RELATIONSHIPS WITH JOURNALISTS AND BROADCASTERS

Most organisations invest in public relations, retaining a company to promote and maintain their 'image' or reputation. Reputation relates to your bottom line, and even has a quantifiable market value.

If you have a PR agency, it will be part of their job to seek out those correspondents and broadcasters who have an interest in your area, and to keep them briefed on new developments. A good relationship of this kind can be invaluable, as it increases the individual's understanding of your business. Just sending out press releases is never enough, the press and media have to have someone they can talk to on a regular basis. That relationship will be stronger if it is based on trust, rather than hype, or the PR person trying to pull the wool over the media's eyes.

Planning ahead

Newspapers and news programmes rely heavily on future planning. They hold editorial meetings every day (for dailies) or every week. At that stage the diary is consulted, and every notable event considered for coverage. If you are doing something noteworthy, your PR company should ensure that at least the diaries know the event is coming up.

CHOOSING A MEDIA TRAINER

When your news coverage gets to the stage of you being invited for interview, you may well begin to feel the need for training to put your point over on radio or television. The PR company may offer to help, but is more likely to recommend a good media training outfit.

Ask a number of questions before choosing a media trainer:

Will the training take place in real studios, or simply with a camera set-up?
A good media trainer should offer both.

What is the quality of the trainer, and have they relevant knowledge of news values?
You need to see not just the potted biographies of people on the team, but to know who will be there when your people are trained. Look out for the posts held: do the broadcasters have editorial and production experience, as well as simply presenting? Presenters do not usually make any decisions about programme content or who is to be interviewed; they may not even decide the angle and focus for the interview.

How many trainers take part?
One trainer to ten participants suggests there will be a lot
of lecturing and not much practical work. Ask for a typical
course outline.

Are the course aims clearly stated?
Trainees who have never been on radio and television
have different needs from more experienced colleagues;
look for evidence that a company offers both fundamental
and advanced or 'refresher' courses.

*How much expertise does the team have in training senior
managers?*
Journalists and broadcasters are not necessarily any good
at teaching adults. Look for some background in tutoring
senior managers, perhaps in a management context.

Are all courses regularly evaluated?
Any decent trainer will evaluate every course as
objectively as possible, and ask for informal feedback too.

What sorts of clients has the company helped?
This is a crucial test. Make sure to see the client list. You
should also be able to consult previous clients for a
reference.

*Has the company a wider range of competences which you
can draw upon?*
Some media trainers may also be able to offer help in
placing articles or getting on to programmes, crisis
preparedness advice and other general promotional
activities, in response to client demand.

EVALUATING YOUR INTERVIEWS

Just as, no doubt, you have some means of estimating the
value of your PR support, it should be possible to judge
the impact of your own interviews. A good media training
company will do this for you, but in brief, look out for:

- The number of questions you were asked.

- Total length of full interview.

- The times when you managed to get over a key message.

- Whether you managed to say anything about your company or its mission (in as natural a way as possible, of course).

- Degree to which messages were clearly conveyed.

- If the interview was hostile, the extent to which you turned round the perceptions of interviewer and audience.

CASE STUDIES

Carol talks too soon

Carol has an old university friend Mandy, who now works as a journalist. They meet for a drink after work and Carol, after a couple of glasses of wine, starts to tell her about Softly, Softly's new product, the electronic purse.

Mandy instantly sees the possibility for a feature article, and starts to pump Carol. Before too long she has elicited all the important facts. 'Carol,' she asks as they depart 'do you have any objection to me writing this up as an article for the *Times* business section?'

'Well of course I do,' says Carol 'what I told you was entirely off the record. You must have realised that.'

'But it would be a good plug for your company, surely.'

Carol is shocked and worried. But Mandy is a very old friend and she accepts the timing is wrong and agrees to do nothing. 'But be more careful in future' she warns 'nothing is really ever off the record.'

John refuses an interview

John is normally very happy to talk to the press, and has good relationships with most of 'his' health correspondents. He has been asked to join a panel on a late night news show, discussing government proposals to move elderly patients from acute hospital beds into private nursing homes, to prevent 'bed blocking': the tying up of expensive, acute care beds by elderly people.

John has discussed the matter extensively with his Chair and Chief Executive, and all are agreed it is a rather political matter, and one on which their Trust's view is no different from any others. John explains this to his journalistic contact, but promises that when another issue comes up, on which John's Trust has something useful to say, he will be only too glad to oblige.

Lesley regrets accepting an invitation

Lesley has become very confident now in her media interviews. She always gives a good account of herself and her charity, and is increasingly sought after by radio and TV programmes.

She agrees to go on *Randy Andy's Friday Night*, a rather raunchy show going out from East Anglia after 10 o'clock on a Friday. (She was rather tempted by the free flight to Cambridge, because she could visit her daughter there.)

It is a show where guests vie with each other to get a word in edgeways, and when Lesley realises the nature of the programme she simply decides not to push herself forward. She is not called on to speak, but still does not arrive at her daughter's flat until the early hours. Lesley is now very clear that she will never again accept an invitation to go on a show she has never watched herself. However, no harm was done to Lesley or her charity.

DEALING WITH THE MEDIA: THE BRIEF GUIDE

Reactive

- Take it seriously.

- Off or on the record?

- Understand what the journalist wants.
- Prepare (call them back).
- Establish three key points.
- Use ordinary language.
- Speak with enthusiasm.

Proactive

- Topicality – a 'peg' or new development.
- A clear story – write the headline!
- Short press release (one side of paper).
- Include key messages.
- Inform two to three weeks in advance.
- Offer interviewees, and if possible 'human examples'.

Have no fear of TV or radio interviews. Be relaxed but alert. The reporters usually want you to perform well. Talk to the reporter, not the microphone or camera. Imagine he/she knows very little about the subject. Be concise and to the point. Try to put your main point across in the first answer. Always be courteous and helpful.

The main points

Use key messages

KISS – keep it simple

Enthusiasm!

(*Rick Thompson, August 1998*)

Glossary

Advertorial. Neither purely editorial copy nor just an advert; where the distinction between the two is blurred.

Angle/peg. Key link to news story or time element which makes a story newsworthy.

Attribution. Linking information or quote to original source.

Bulletin. Short news item on TV or radio.

Byline. The name of the journalist who has written the story.

Caption. Line of print under a photograph which explains it.

Chequebook journalism. Large sum of money paid for story, generally salacious.

Chief sub. Senior journalist in charge of sub-editors.

Clippings/cuttings. Past articles on which journalists base their research for a story.

Copy. The words produced by journalists.

Deadline. Time/date or hour by which journalist has to submit the copy for a story.

Diary. List of upcoming events which a newspaper or programme will cover by providing a journalist.

Diary. Report of an event coming unsolicited from a reporter.

Doorstepping. Literally standing outside front door of house or office, lying in wait for someone to emerge.

Editor. The most senior person on the editorial team; legally responsible for all the contents. In overall charge of the editorial content of a newspaper or programme.

Editorial. Any matter which is not advertising.

Embargo. Time before which an organisation issuing material – usually a press release – does not want the information to be published, usually found on press releases. Assumes media will respect. A request not to publish before a certain date/hour.

Feature story/news story. Mutually exclusive terms. A feature tends to be longer and carry more background information. A news story will be more centred on the facts: who, what, where, when, why.

(To) File a story. To submit copy.

Headline. Written by sub-editor, not by journalist who supplied the copy.

Intro. First paragraph of a story; the first two or three lines after the headline.

Kill. To drop a story; a freelance will want a 'kill fee' for story not used.

Knocking copy. Negative story.

Leader. The opinion piece in a newspaper; statement of views or opinions by the editor; indicates the political position of the paper or magazine.

Morgue. Press cutting library; holdings of back issues.

Must. Copy that must appear, eg a correction or an apology.

Nib. News in brief: short news item(s); under 100 words.

Off the record. Statements made to a journalist on the understanding (or in the belief) that they will not be used other than as background; not for publication but for background only.

PA. The Press Association. Supplies other newspapers and news outlets with factual accounts.

Pick up. Freebies: free information or photographs/pictures supplied for journalists' use at press conferences.

Pix. Pictures or photographs.

Press day. The day a publication closes and goes to the printers; the last day for news (doesn't apply to daily, but to weekly or bi-weekly publications).

Producer. The person responsible for putting a programme on the air.

Pull quote. A quote selected by the sub-editor and set out in larger typeface.

Quote. Generally a direct verbatim quote from a named source, enclosed in inverted commas.

Reporter. Journalist working on news stories. In broadcasting the person responsible for compiling writing as well as presenting the piece.

Ring-round. Story based on a series of telephone calls.

Script. Copy in broadcast journalist terms.

Snap. Early summary by news agency of an important developing story.

Soundbite. A few words or short comment extracted from an interview.

Story. A potential news item which needs to be made to stand up, ie backed by facts.

Sub-editor/sub. Person who edits the copy supplied by reporters, writes the headlines and captions for pictures; journalist who checks, corrects, rewrites copy, writes headlines and captions, checks proofs. On newspapers, also responsible for layout. Checks facts, names, places. Corrects grammar and spelling. Ensures in-house style is observed. Makes sure text fits into space. May rewrite some or all of the copy. Checks the story is legally safe. Writes captions and headlines. Selects pull quotes.

Tots. Triumph over tragedy story.

Unattributable. Statements made to a journalist on the understanding that they will not be attributed to the source on publication. Should not be possible to trace the comments back to the source.

Vox pop. Series of quotes from the general public on particular theme.

Further Reading

The Craft of the Media Interview, Dennis Barker (1988).
Face the Press: Managing the media interview, John B.J.
   Lidstone (Nicholas Brealey Publishing).
Hitting the Headlines, Stephen White, Peter Evans, Chris
   Mihill and Maryon Tyson (The British Psychological
   Society).
How to Handle Media Interviews, Andrew Boyd (Mercury).
Mastering the News Media Interview: How to succeed,
   Stephen C. Rafe (Harper Business, 1991).
Media Interview Techniques, Peter Tidman and H. Lloyd
   Slater (McGraw-Hill).
Press Here! Managing the media for free publicity, Annie
   Gurton (Prentice Hall, 1998).
Surviving the Media Jungle, Diana Ross (Pitman).
*Uninvited Guests: The intimate secrets of television and
   radio*, Laurie Taylor, (Coronet).
Your Message and the Media, Linda Fairbrother (Nicholas
   Brealey Publishing, 1993).

Useful Addresses

NATIONAL DAILIES

Daily Mail, 2 Derry Street, Kensington, London W8 5TT.
  Tel: (020) 7938 6000. Editor: Paul Dacre.
Daily Star, 245 Blackfriars Road, London SE1 9UX. Tel:
  (020) 7921 5000. Editor: Peter Hill.
Daily Telegraph, 1 Canada Square, Canary Wharf, London
  E14 5DT. Tel: (020) 7538 5000. News Editor: Charles
  Moore.
The Express, 245 Blackfriars Road, London SE1 9UX. Tel:
  (020) 7928 8000. Editor: Chris Williams.
Financial Times, 1 Southwark Bridge, London SE1 9HL.
  Tel: (020) 7873 3000. Editor: Andrew Gowers.
The Guardian, 119 Farringdon Road, London EC1R 3ER.
  Tel: (020) 7278 2332. Editor: Alan Rusbridger.
Independent, 1 Canada Square, Canary Wharf, London
  E14 5DL. Tel: (020) 7293 2047. Editor: Simon Kelner.
The Mirror, 1 Canada Square, Canary Wharf, London E14
  5AP. Tel: (020) 7293 3000. Editor: Piers Morgan.
The Sun, 1 Virginia Street, Wapping, London E1 9BD. Tel:
  (020) 7782 4000. Editor: David Yelland.
The Times, 1 Pennington Street, Wapping, London E1
  9XN. Tel: (020) 7782 5000. Editor: Robert Thomson.

BROADCASTING ORGANISATIONS

BBC Network Television, Television Centre, Wood Lane,
  London W12 7RJ. Tel: (020) 8743 8000.
BBC World Service, Bush House, PO Box 76, London
  WC2B 4PH. Tel: (020) 7240 3456.

BBC Network Radio, Broadcasting House, Portland Place, London W1A 1AA. Tel: (020) 7580 4468.

BBC Scotland, Broadcasting House, Queen Margaret Drive, Glasgow G12 8DG. Tel: (0141) 338 2000.

BBC Wales, Broadcasting House, Llantrisant Road, Llandaff, Cardiff CF5 2YQ. Tel: (029) 2057 2888.

BBC Northern Ireland, Broadcasting House, Ormeau Avenue, Belfast BT2 8HQ. Tel: (01232) 338000.

ITN (Independent Television News), 200 Grays Inn Road, London WC1X 8XZ. Tel: (020) 7833 3000.

Anglia Television, Anglia House, Norwich, Norfolk NR1 3JG. Tel: (01603) 615151.

Border Television, Durranhill, Carlisle, Cumbria CA1 3NT. Tel: (01228) 525101.

Central Broadcasting, Central House, Broad Street, Birmingham B1 2JP. Tel: (0121) 643 9898.

Channel Television, Television Centre Le Pouquelaye, St Helier, Jersey, Channel Islands JE2 3ZD. Tel: (01534) 816816.

GMTV, London Television Centre, Upper Ground, London SE1 9TT. Tel: (020) 7827 7000.

Grampian Television, Queen's Cross, Aberdeen, Grampian AB15 4XJ. Tel: (01224) 84686.

Granada Television, Quay Street, Manchester M60 9EA. Tel: (0161) 832 7211.

London Weekend Television, London Television Centre, Upper Ground, London SE1 9LT. Tel: (020) 7620 1620.

Meridian Broadcasting, Television Centre, Northam, Southampton, Hants SO14 0PZ. Tel: (023) 8022 2555.

Scottish Television, Cowcaddens, Glasgow G2 3PR. Tel: (0141) 300 3000.

Tyne Tees Television, City Road, Newcastle-upon-Tyne NE1 2AL. Tel: (0191) 261 0181.

UTV (Ulster Television), Ormeau Road, Belfast BT7 1EB. Tel: (028) 9032 8122.

Westcountry Television, Langage Science Park, Western Wood Way, Baham, Plymouth PL7 5BG. Tel: (01752) 333333.

Yorkshire Television, Kirkstall Road, Leeds, West Yorks
LS3 1JS. Tel: (0113) 243 8283.
Channel 4, 124 Horseferry Road, London SW1P 2TX. Tel:
(020) 7306 8351.
Channel 5 Broadcasting, 22 Longacre, London WC2E
9LY. Tel: (020) 7430 4100.
BSkyB, 6 Centaurs Business Park, Grant Way, Isleworth,
Middlesex TW7 5QD. Tel: (020) 7705 3000.

MEDIA TRAINING COMPANIES

Hillside Training, Jean Gurteen. Tel: (020) 8950 7919.
InterMedia Training. Tel: (020)7223 2300.
Media Counsellors. Tel: (0118) 988 0244.
Media Interviews. Tel: (01225) 338922.
Media Minds Ltd, Judith Byrne. Tel: (01993) 898559.
www.media-minds.co.uk

Index